3D Delineation:

A modernisation of drawing methodology for field archaeology

Justin J.L. Kimball

Archaeopress Publishing Ltd
Gordon House
276 Banbury Road
Oxford OX2 7ED

www.archaeopress.com

ISBN 978 1 78491 305 2
ISBN 978 1 78491 306 9 (e-Pdf)

© Archaeopress and J J L Kimball 2016

All rights reserved. No part of this book may be reproduced or transmitted, in any form or by any means, electronic, mechanical, photocopying or otherwise, without the prior written permission of the copyright owners.

Printed and bound in Great Britain by Marston Book Services Ltd, Oxfordshire

Contents

Abstract v
Preface vi
1 – Introduction 1
2 – State of the Art 3
3 – Theory 11
4 – Methodology 14
4.1 – Review of Established Methodologies and Associated Technologies 14
4.2 – Introduction to Utilised Technologies 16
    4.2.1 – Camera Systems 17
    4.2.2 – Adobe Photoshop Lightroom 5.4 19
    4.2.3 – Agisoft's Photoscan 1.0.4 20
    4.2.4 – EDM Total Station 22
    4.2.5 – ArcGIS 10.2.1 23
4.3 – Limitations 23
5 – Experiment: 3D Delineation 24
5.1 – General Background of Uppåkra 24
5.2 – Documentation Methodology at Uppåkra since 2011 25
5.3 – State of the Art: 3D Modelling at Uppåkra 26
5.4 – Experiment Overview 27
5.5 – Experiment Methodology 27
5.6 – Results Concerning 3D Archaeological Drawings 31
6 – Discussion 45
6.1 – Statement of Perceived Impact 49
    6.1.1 – Guidelines and Symbologies for 3D Archaeological Drawing 50
6.2 – Cautions and Limitations 53
6.3 – Concerns Regarding the Photographic Process 56
7 – Conclusion 61
8 – Acknowledgments 63
9 – References 64
9.1 – Literary Sources 64
9.2 – Online Sources 67
9.3 – Multimedia Sources 68

List of Figures

FIGURE 1 – A drawing detailing the various line types as established by the Museum of London Archaeology for use in the single context method of archaeological drawing. (Redrawn by J.J.L. Kimball 2014, symbology established by Museum of London Archaeology Service 1994). 5

FIGURE 2 – An example of early archaeological photography; pictured is the apex of the excavation of the Oseberg Ship, Norway. (Photograph © Kulturhistorisk Museum, UiO 2014). 6

FIGURE 3 – Another example of early archaeological photography; pictured are the excavators and archaeologists, in the background the Oseberg Ship, Norway. (Photograph © Kulturhistorisk Museum, UiO 2014). 7

FIGURE 4 – A visual depiction of the pipeline of technologies used in this work's experiment. Included in the above list are the following: (A) the physical archaeological object; (B) digital SLR camera; (C) control points for geospatial recording; (D) RAW image format; (E) Adobe Photoshop Lightroom; (F) JPG image format; (G) EDM Total station; (H) Agisoft's Photoscan; (I) ESRI's 3D GIS ArcScene; (J) ESRI shapefiles [points, polylines, and polygons]; (K) ArcScene 2D output formats [e.g. JPG and PDF]; (L) ArcScene 3D output format [e.g. WRL]; (M) ESRI attribute tables; and (N) ArcScene table output formats [e.g. Microsoft Excel]. (Image by J.J.L. Kimball 2014; all logos and associated concepts are copyright of their respective companies). 18

FIGURE 5 – (Screen-captures of a 3D model) Steps in MSR production with Photoscan; (top) estimation of internal camera parameters and camera projections; (left) dense-point cloud; (right) mesh. (Image by J.J.L. Kimball 2014; 3D model by J.J.L. Kimball 2014) 20

FIGURE 6 – (Screen-capture of a 3D Model) The final stage of MSR—a photorealistic 3D model of the runestone DR 330 "Gårdstångastenen 2" located in Lund, Sweden. (Image by J.J.L. Kimball 2014; 3D model by J.J.L. Kimball 2014). 21

FIGURE 7 – A photograph looking southward over top of several of the 2013 excavation trenches. (Photograph © J.J.L. Kimball 2013). 25

FIGURE 8 – A photograph from one of the acquisition campaigns around Trench 5; note the markers along the edges of the trench. (Photograph © J.J.L. Kimball 2013). 28

FIGURE 9 – (Screen-capture) The 3D models located within their proper geospatial locations within ArcScene. (Image by J.J.L. Kimball 2014; 3D models and GIS implementation by N. Dell'Unto and the Department of Archaeology and Ancient History, Lund University 2013). 29

FIGURE 10 – A short example of some of the database fields and values during the input stage. (Image by J.J.L. Kimball 2014). 30

FIGURE 11 – A photograph displaying some of the complexities faced in Trench 5. (Photograph © J.J.L. Kimball 2013). 31

FIGURE 12 – (Screen-capture of a 3D Model/3D drawing) this example show the general range of complexities to be drawn; the green polyline denotes a small and relatively non-complex layer whereas the blue polyline denotes a large and complex layer. (Image by J.J.L. Kimball 2014; 3D drawings by J.J.L. Kimball 2014; 3D model by N. Dell'Unto 2013). 32

FIGURE 13 – (Screen-capture of 3D models/3D drawing) Here the same model and drawings as are displayed in the above figure are shown in their geospatial relation to other 3D models within the GIS. (Image by J.J.L. Kimball 2014; 3D drawings by J.J.L. Kimball 2014; 3D Models and GIS implementation by N. Dell'Unto and the Department of Archaeology and Ancient History, Lund University 2013). 32

FIGURE 14 – (Composite screen-capture image of a 3D Model/3D drawing) An example showing the development of the drawing process overtop of the stone-packing layer. Notice the increase of orange polylines between the top and bottom images. (Image by J.J.L. Kimball 2014; 3D model/3D drawings by J.J.L. Kimball 2014). 33

FIGURE 15 – (Composite screen-capture image of a 3D model showing/3D drawing) (i) stone-packing with no drawing; (ii) stone-packing delineated by polylines; and (iii) stone-packing visualised only as polygons. (Images by J.J.L. Kimball 2014; 3D models/3D drawings by J.J.L. Kimball 2014). 34

FIGURE 16 – This image shows a comparison between traditional methods and digital methods. The top image is a 3D representation of the stone-packing layer; to the left is a hand-drawn plan; and to the right is a 3D drawing in plan perspective. (Image by J.J.L. Kimball 2014; 3D Models/3D drawing by J.J.L. Kimball 2014; Hand-Drawn Plan by J. Lundin 2013). 35

FIGURE 17 – (Screen-capture of 3D model/3D drawing) a composite image showing the relationship between a 3D model and its 3D drawing. Starting in the bottom left corner is an oval shape of the 3d model without any drawings; the next oval shape outward is of the 3D model and its complex polygon geometry in relation to the simple polygons of the 3D drawing—notice that that much of the pink 3D drawings are hidden by the 3D model itself. The outer region shows the 3D drawings only without the 3D model. (Image by J.J.L. Kimball 2014; 3D models/3D drawings by J.J.L. Kimball 2014). 36

FIGURE 18 – (Screen-capture of a 3D model/3D drawing; section perspective) This image was captured during the drawing process. At first glance, one might believe that these nodes have been accurately placed upon the surface of the model, allowing for the successful development of a polygon. (Image by J.J.L. Kimball 2014; 3D model/3D drawings by J.J.L. Kimball 2014). 37

FIGURE 19 – (Screen-capture of a 3D model/3D drawing; Slightly oblique plan perspective) This image was captured after the drawing process had been completed. On closer inspection, some nodes have 'lifted' off of the surface, creating a very tedious task to relocate them into their intended positions. Two Breaks in the polygon can also be seen centre to centre right (image by J.J.L. Kimball 2014; 3D model/3D drawings by J.J.L. Kimball 2014). 37

FIGURE 20 – (Screen-capture of a 3D drawing; section perspective) This image was captured after the drawing process had been completed. A major drawback of drawing in 3D with polygons is that the polygon is projected as individually segregated pieces—note the Shading differences and most significantly the seven white spaces between. (image by J.J.L. Kimball 2014; 3D Drawing by J.J.L. Kimball 2014). 38

FIGURE 21 – (Screen-capture of a 3D model/3D drawing) the only examples where polygons were used successfully to distinguish between layers. The model itself has been made more transparent to help the reader see the complete extents of the section drawings (image by J.J.L. Kimball 2014; 3D drawings by J.J.L. Kimball 2014; 3D model by N. Dell'Unto). 38

FIGURE 22 – (Screen-capture of 3D Drawings). This image shows a variety of contexts and sections projected in the same environment and in relation to one another. (image and 3D drawing by J.J.L. Kimball 2014. Reference 3D model by N. Dell'Unto 2013) 40

FIGURE 23 – (Screen-capture) Here are two examples of the current drawing methodology at Uppåkra. [left] a plan drawing of contexts acquired via total station; [right] a digitised section drawing. By design these drawings must be viewed out of context from one another (Images by Söderberg et al. 2014). 40

FIGURE 24 – (Screen-capture of a 3D Model/3D Drawing) An example of chronological layering: a model of a younger phase of the excavation is reduced in transparency and superimposed over top of a drawing of rock-packing (an older phase). (Image and 3D drawing by J.J.L. Kimball 2014; 3D model by N. Dell'Unto). 41

FIGURE 25 – (Screen-capture of 3D models) Another example of chronological layering: this time the overlaying 3D model is significantly reduced in transparency so that the base model can be seen. To help delineate the location of the overlay model's features, a drawn outline has been provided. (Image by J.J.L. Kimball 2014; Base 3D model by J.J.L. Kimball 2014; Overlay 3D model by N. Dell'Unto)...41

FIGURE 26 – (Screen-capture of 3D model/3D Drawing) Here the 3D drawing has been slightly transparent and overlayed on top of the first 3D model of trench 5. (Image and 3D drawing by J.J.L. Kimball 2014; 3D model by N. Dell'Unto)..42

FIGURE 27 – (Screen-capture of 3D model/3D drawing) The top image shows completed 3D drawing for the second 3D model of Trench 5. The bottom image shows a transparent overlay of the 3D drawing overtop of 3D model. (Images by J.J.L. Kimball 2014; 3D models/3D drawings by J.J.L. Kimball 2014). 43

FIGURE 28 – (Screen-capture of 3D models) 3D drawings of the latest stage of excavations in Trench 5 displayed in their geospatial relation to other 3D models within the GIS. (Image and 3D drawing by J.J.L. Kimball 2014; Base 3D model for Trench 5 by J.J.L. Kimball 2014, all other 3D Models and GIS implementation by N. Dell'Unto and the Department of Archaeology and Ancient History, Lund University 2013). 44

FIGURE 29 – (Screen-capture of a 3D drawing) One of the measure tool features in Arcscene: here the tool has been used to measure diagonally across the stone-packing layer which provides a result of 1.959 meters across. (Image by J.J.L. Kimball 2014; Reference 3D model/3D drawing by J.J.L. Kimball 2014). 47

FIGURE 30 – (Composite screen-capture of 3D models) Shown here is how ArcScene projects lines. the top image is a simple line that is easily projected; bottom is a complex line which ArcScene cannot project. For both images, the corresponding line symbology is denoted in the bottom right corner of the related image (Image by J.J.L. Kimball 2014; 3D models by J.J.L. Kimball). 51

FIGURE 31 – A proposed standard symbology for 3D drawing: (A) limit of excavation; (B) extent of context; (C) edge of context truncated by latter intrusion; and (D) extent uncertain. (Image by J.J.L. Kimball 2014). 52

FIGURE 32 – (Screen-capture of 3D drawing) Despite placing the nodes in a logical sequence, the resulting polygon is not correctly projected. Instead of a single polygon, ArcScene breaks it into nine different pieces or 'parts'—each with its own specific set of nodes. (Image by J.J.L. Kimball 2014; 3D model/3D drawing by J.J.L. Kimball 2014). 55

FIGURE 33 – (Photograph) Buckets, strings, finds markers, range poles—all of these must be cleared from the site to ensure as clean a model as possible. (Photograph © J.J.L. Kimball 2013). 57

FIGURE 34 – (Screen-capture of a 3D Model) The consequence of not preparing the site by removal of items non-essential for the photographic process. Visible are multiple projections of one string, a neon strip of tape, and a hint of red in the corner of the trench from a range pole. (Image by J.J.L. Kimball 2014; 3D model by J.J.L. Kimball 2014). 58

FIGURE 35 – (Screen-capture of a 3D Model) The blue circle highlights a partial boot print that is forever immortalised in this 3D digital model. (Image by J.J.L. Kimball 2014; 3D model by N. Dell'Unto)......59

Abstract

A recent trend concerning archaeological research has focused on producing a real-time methodology for 3D digital models as archaeological documentation within the excavation setting. While such methodologies have now firmly been established, what remains is to examine how 3D models can be integrated more fully alongside other forms of archaeological documentation. This work explored one avenue by developing a method that combines the interpretative power of traditional archaeological drawings and the realistic visualisation capacity of 3D digital models. An experiment was initiated during archaeological excavations at Uppåkra, Sweden where photographic data was captured to produce 3D digital models through Photoscan. These models were geospatially located within ESRI's 3D GIS ArcScene where shapefile editing tools were used to draw overtop of their surfaces in three-dimensions. All drawings closely followed the single context method of drawing, were allotted context numbers, and given descriptive geodatabase attributes. This methodology resulted in the further integration of 3D models alongside other forms of archaeological documentation. The drawings increased the communicative powers of archaeological interpretation by enabling the information to be disseminated in a 3D environment alongside other formats of data that would have otherwise been disconnected in 2D space. Finally, the database attributes permitted the drawings complete integration within the geodatabase, thereby making them available for query and other analytical procedures. Archaeological information is three-dimensional; therefore, archaeologists must begin to approach documentation bearing this in mind. This technique has demonstrated that 3D models are a fluidic form of documentation allowing for accurate preservation of archaeology while enabling new forms of data to be derived all within a limited amount of time. Archaeologists must begin to affect change towards embracing 3D models and their associated applications as a standard tool within the excavator's toolbox.

Keywords: 3D modelling; multi-view stereo reconstruction; MSR; archaeological drawing; 3D drawing; field archaeology; excavation methodology; excavation documentation; archaeological photography; transparency; reconstruction; 3D/4D GIS.

Cover Image: (A still image of 3D models and 3D drawings) Presented here is a composite image showing multiple 3D models and 3D drawings from the same perspective in a 3D GIS environment. From upper left corner to lower right corner: 1) 3D model of an earlier phase of excavation of an oven feature in Trench 5, Uppåkra; 2) the same 3D model as before, reduced in transparency to reveal the 3D delineation of archaeological features that were 'at-the-time' hidden beneath the clay layer (an example of chronological—4D—layering; 3) another example showing chronological layering, this time solely with 3D drawings of the clay horseshoe-shape and the underlying stone-packing layer; 4) an image retaining the 3D polygon drawing of the horseshoe-shaped clay layer superimposed over top of the last phase of excavation (stone-packing layer); and 5) a final example of chronological layering where only the 3D polyline is visible over the 3D model representing the last phase of excavations. (Image by J.J.L. Kimball 2014; 3D Drawings by J.J.L. Kimball 2014; Base 3D model by J.J.L. Kimball 2014; Overlay 3D model by N. Dell'Unto).

Back Cover Image: (Screen-capture of 3D model/3D drawing) The top image shows completed 3D drawing for the second 3D model of Trench 5. The bottom image shows a transparent overlay of the 3D drawing overtop of 3D model. (Images by J.J.L. Kimball 2014; 3D models/3D drawings by J.J.L. Kimball 2014).

Preface

The research and its results contained herein represent an original and independent thesis work by the author Justin J.L. Kimball, under the supervision of Dr Nicolo Dell'Unto, for the degree of Master of Arts in Archaeology from the Department of Archaeology and Ancient History, Lund University (Sweden) and was awarded in 2014.

The original version of this work, in thesis format, may be found on the Lund University Publications (LUP) Student Papers website—the hyperlink to the search catalogue found in the footnote below.[1]

In accordance with *Archaeopress*, the work contained within this documented has been modified to reflect the publisher's stylistic guidelines and publication standards. Apart from these changes, the content material remains largely unaltered from the original version.

---

[1] Lund University Publications Student Papers search site: https://lup.lub.lu.se/student-papers/search

1 – Introduction

Field archaeology has always been a discipline that depends greatly upon technology and the way those technologies are used in order to achieve knowledge of archaeological material (Jensen 2012: 12-13). Such a fact has become reaffirmed in the last two and a half decades as digital technologies have increasingly made their presence evident throughout archaeology. This particular influx has been of tremendous benefit in that digital technologies have opened new possibilities through which new paths have been pioneered. Following such opportunities, archaeologists have now acquired the ability to look upon the excavation with new light: the application of digital technology not only enables new forms of data for analyses, it also facilitates all stages of acquisition, management, and post-processing—including not just digital, but traditional forms of data as well. Research into digital technologies thus enables an exciting and promising avenue for the documentation and understanding of archaeological resources. While an increased dependence upon digital technologies does not mark a replacement of traditional archaeological tools, it is important to recognise that digital technologies are able to play an important supplementary role—one where, through our potential to acquire and interpret both traditional and newer forms of data, the conclusions of an archaeological investigation are made more accurately, expeditious, and fruitful.

It must be recognised, however, that digital technologies are in a continuous state of development and thus these technologies, whether indirectly or directly, are also developing as viable components towards the production of archaeological knowledge. In turn, this signifies that there are yet many aspects to be explored regarding the theoretical and methodological aspects of digital technology itself and its role in concert alongside of their more traditional counterparts in archaeology. Therefore, the pronounced youth of digital technologies sets forth a profound challenge for archaeologists. Only through an all-encompassing, deliberate, and objectified amelioration of digital methodologies will these technologies be able to find their place within archaeology—a deployment where their strengths are used efficiently and, more importantly, in an archaeologically relevant manner—and further towards the development of standards aimed at achieving comprehension over targeted archaeological material and the ability to disseminate the resulting knowledge (Campana 2014: 7-8).

One of these more recent trends in the use of digital technologies in archaeology has been the introduction of and the increasing interest placed upon 3D digital data technologies. The impact is ultimately tied to advances in computer technologies: the increase in power and decrease in cost has made 'luxuries' such as 3D modelling more attractive. This in turn has opened up a typology of data that is so new and exciting that its role has not yet been firmly cemented within archaeology. Thus, both a heightened awareness and a desire to solidify a place for 3D digital data technologies have created an interest to pursue these technologies more thoroughly. In field archaeology for example, a continual stream of research papers has been published over the past decade where 3D models have been used to capture and generate archaeological knowledge. Some of these experiments are significant as they have been attempted within the timeframe of the excavation itself. These mark important milestones as they have shed light upon the value that 3D models present for archaeology.[1]

Thus, the methodology described and developed in this work has sought to contribute towards the exploration of innovative applications for 3D data in field archaeology. It has specifically addressed the question: in what other manners can 3D models be used in the comprehension, interpretation, and

---

[1] By design, the 2D medium that this work has been written on frustrates the ability to visually demonstrate certain aspects about the 3D objects discussed. This has been somewhat circumvented through a webpage that the reader may visit for additional 3D visual information (e.g. images, videos, and 3D PDFs). Wherever applicable, a link, such as the one below, will be provided in a footnote to direct the reader to the website containing additional visual media. https://sites.google.com/site/justinjlkimball/masters-data

visualisation of archaeological materials? In other words, beyond simply creating and visualising 3D models, how can these models aid field archaeologists in making explicit what has been identified as archaeologically-relevant? Utilising some of the methodologies and techniques produced in previous studies, this work has demonstrated a different approach in using 3D surface models that builds upon the strengths offered through this technology. Furthermore, this application for 3D models has been shown to fit seamlessly alongside of other traditional excavation tools—a combination that facilitates the production and communication of archaeological knowledge. These methodologies have the potential to provide researchers with unique and powerful perspectives and therefore must be considered as prosperous ventures for future research and deployment within field archaeology.

2 – State of the Art

Central to numerous state of the art sections is the exploration of technology and its impacts within the area of study. 'Technology' is a key concept throughout this work and, thus, it is relevant to establish a clear understanding of what the term actually encompasses. A general perspective comes from the *Oxford Dictionary of English* which defines technology as "the application of scientific knowledge [in the form of machinery and/or devices] for practical purposes" (Stevenson 2010). If one were to narrow the perspective into pursuing a more archaeologically-relevant definition for technology, the *Concise Oxford Dictionary of Archaeology* states that technology is "the application of knowledge to facilitate the *obtaining and transformation of natural materials*" and that "technology involves the creation of material instruments . . . *used in human interactions with nature*" [emphasis mine] (Darvill 2009). This definition is decidedly more accurate regarding the role of technology within archaeology.

As human beings, we explore and experience our world through our highly-sophisticated sensory organs. However, while we may assume an all-encompassing comprehension of the world around us through these senses, we are actually quite confined by the limitations of those organs. Technology, however, presents a means through which we are able to *augment* our bodies and/or senses, thereby allowing us to realise what would otherwise be difficult or even impossible to perceive. Such a concept is easy to illustrate through how archaeologists use technology to enhance certain aspects of the real-world. Take, for example, the archaeological use of remote sensing. From a very general perspective, remote sensing may be understood as "the acquisition and measurement of information about certain properties of phenomena, objects, or materials by a recording device not in physical contact with the features under surveillance" (Khorram et al. 2012: 2; cf. also Schowengerdt 2007: 2; Wiseman and El-Baz 2007: 1). To maintain the distance from the subject, these recording instruments are commonly affixed to mobile platforms such as airplanes and satellites (Khorram et al. 2012: 2) although other types of platforms, especially within archaeological settings, may also be utilised such as kites, balloons, and unmanned aerial vehicles (UAVs) (cf. Eisenbeiss 2009). The instruments used are specially attuned to receive specific propagated signals within a typology, such as those within the electromagnetic spectrum (Khorram et al. 2012: 2; Parcak 2009: 42-44; Schowengerdt 2007: 2). In essence, these sensors permit the operator to 'see' certain signals (e.g. gamma, x-ray, ultraviolet, near and middle infrared, thermal infrared, microwave, and radio) that would otherwise be invisible to the naked eye.

Bearing this example and the previous definitions in mind, I propose that a more accurate definition of technology—where technology is more explicitly understood as *a tool within* archaeology—might be described as the development and application of scientific knowledge as implements intended to facilitate, augment, and/or transcend biological limitations with an overarching goal to enable interaction with a variety of archaeologically-relevant materials. With the definition of technology now thoroughly explored and established, the evolution of technology within archaeology ending in the current state of the art may now be summarised.

The primary goal of archaeology is, of course, chiefly concerned with understanding our human past. In order to achieve this, archaeologists must have access to data and the primary mode of acquiring such data is through the process of excavation: where archaeological material—obtainable through no other means—is literally unearthed from its encasement within the ground (Barker 1993: 13). In its earliest form, archaeology was aimed towards recovering only artefacts. Thus, shovels and mattocks were utilised to clear away earth in order to gain access to those objects. This changed in the 19th century when archaeologists began to focus more on the archaeological site and the information that was contained within. Naturally, this led to the development of the written and drawn records, both of which complement one another and are standards of excavation to this day (Barker 1993; Drewitt 2011; Roskams 2001). Drawn records focus specifically on the production of drawings derived from the measurement of surface features and can be broken down into horizontal ('plan') and vertical ('section' or 'profile') types. The emphasis upon recording features within the site, rather than only focusing upon the collection of artefacts, ultimately impacted the act of excavation. More specifically, in order to accommodate the written and drawn records, excavation had to be conducted in a meticulous and clean manner (Barker 1993: 25). As a result, tools capable of finesse were employed for excavation purposes—the most iconic of course being the trowel. It is important to recognise however that the trowel did not completely supplant the shovel. On the contrary, the trowel was adopted in response to the need to take more care during the excavation process—an aspect that arose with the adoption of newer techniques that in turn inspired new methodologies and resulted in the realisation of new forms of archaeological data.

The increased attention to detail influenced other aspects of the site to be scrutinised. One of particular relevance was the study of the stratigraphic sequence which allowed archaeologists a better understanding of site creation and past activities (Museum of London Archaeological Service 1994). The inspiration for the archaeological study of stratigraphy was borrowed from geology with particular attention paid to the Geological Law of Superposition. In 1973, Edward Harris would amend this law to make it more suitable for archaeology. Thus Harris' (Archaeological) Law of Superposition holds that:

> "In a series of layers and interfacial features, as originally created, the upper units of stratification are younger and the lower are older, for each must have been deposited on, or created by the removal of, a pre-existing mass of archaeological stratification"
>
> E. C. Harris (1997: 30).

Superposition is an important concept because it seeks to understand the relationship between the features and deposits within a site (Harris 1997: 30). More importantly was that this work lead to the development of an excavation methodology named the 'Single Context System.' Intended for use at sites with complex stratifications, this method functions under the knowledge that archaeological sites are formed through actions that either deposit or remove layers. The results of such actions are referred to as 'contexts' and are always either 'sealed' or 'cut' by the context(s) above (Museum of London Archaeological Service 1994). Thus, each individual context is considered important, resulting in the production of large numbers of documents (e.g. drawings—a format central to this work). The methodology for such drawings was standardised in order to ensure they were scientifically valuable. Thus, the act of drawing follows a specific set of guidelines that help to produce 2D geometric representations of the object recorded. In order to facilitate the production of these archaeological drawings, a standardised symbology, called the 'Single Context Planning Method,' was established where specific line types were used to translate 3D archaeological features into a 2D medium. These unique and descriptive lines help to convey important information that would otherwise be difficult to explain in writing (cf. FIGURE 1) and are an industry standard in archaeological practice today.

Another important technology leading towards the current state of the art was the introduction and development of photography within archaeology. Photographic technology presented a powerful tool to archaeologists that, when executed by someone with photographic experience, was able to quickly record a highly-detailed representation of the site. Although photography started out as a way to document the apex of archaeological discovery (cf. FIGURE 2 and FIGURE 3), archaeologists eventually began to record the phases of excavation as the archaeological investigation progressed forward (Drewitt 2011: 131). Later in the 20th century, as photography equipment became more compact and mobile, the photographic record developed into an incredibly important component within archaeological investigations. The increased

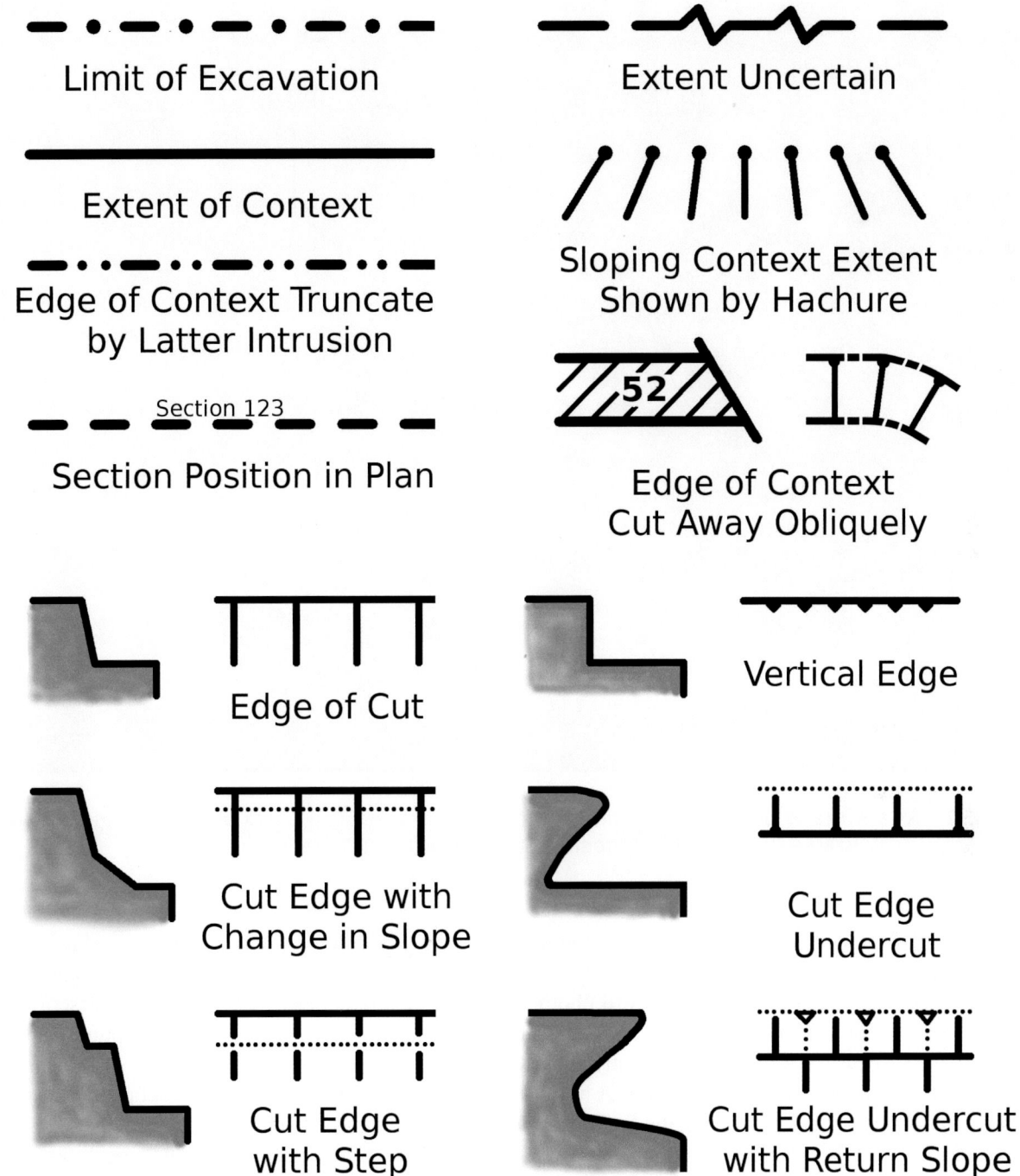

FIGURE 1 – A DRAWING DETAILING THE VARIOUS LINE TYPES AS ESTABLISHED BY THE MUSEUM OF LONDON ARCHAEOLOGY FOR USE IN THE SINGLE CONTEXT METHOD OF ARCHAEOLOGICAL DRAWING. (REDRAWN BY J.J.L. KIMBALL 2014, SYMBOLOGY ESTABLISHED BY MUSEUM OF LONDON ARCHAEOLOGY SERVICE 1994).

FIGURE 2 – AN EXAMPLE OF EARLY ARCHAEOLOGICAL PHOTOGRAPHY; PICTURED IS THE APEX OF THE EXCAVATION OF THE OSEBERG SHIP, NORWAY. (PHOTOGRAPH © KULTURHISTORISK MUSEUM, UiO 2014).

flexibility of this technology influenced the creation of its own methodology, where archaeological features and surfaces were first prepared in order to visually define as much detail as possible for photographic recording (Drewitt 2011: 131). Such record photographs can be broken down into two groups describing the perspective from which they are captured: vertical and oblique (Barker 1993: 181). Vertical photography refers to the suspension of the camera directly above the subject for recording (Barker 1993: 181-182). This form of photography produces an image that has a similar perspective to the archaeological plan drawing. Oblique photography helps to define the features of the site by using various lighting and camera angles to record the contrasts between highlights and shadows. This teases out details that may otherwise be difficult to see (Barker 1993: 182-183), such as the subtleties between individual rocks in a stone-packing or highlighting the edge of a posthole.

It is at this point that an important consideration must be made regarding the role of photographic technology. First, and perhaps most easy to overlook, is that photography threatens to override careful in-the-moment observation and interpretation (Barker 1993: 185-186). In the modern day, this is a particularly relevant concern with fully automatic cameras and, indeed, even cameras attached to nearly every mobile device. Second is in relation to the nature of the photograph which is a static representation of the subject. What is meant by *static*

FIGURE 3 – ANOTHER EXAMPLE OF EARLY ARCHAEOLOGICAL PHOTOGRAPHY; PICTURED ARE THE EXCAVATORS AND ARCHAEOLOGISTS, IN THE BACKGROUND THE OSEBERG SHIP, NORWAY. (PHOTOGRAPH © KULTURHISTORISK MUSEUM, UiO 2014).

is that the photograph produced is dependent on a number of variables ranging from photographic variables like camera and lighting angles, to archaeological variables such as time of archaeological exposure (e.g. variables concerning moisture levels, colour fastness of dyes and paints, etc.). In other words, there is no way to exactly replicate these values after the photos have been shot and the excavation has moved forward. Finally, while it is true that photographs provide a highly detailed representation of the subjected captured, there are specific limitations that are most visible when compared against other documentation types—such as drawings. As described above, drawings are a representation of the geometrical characteristics within a site. Drawings furthermore must be done in the field and in front of the subject of study. Thus, the archaeologist who draws geometrical characteristics does so because she/he 'interprets' these as being a relevant component relating to the overall interpretation of the site. Photography on the other hand, is a type of 'survey' in that the camera indiscriminately records everything that is within its field of view. In this sense, photographs provide a 'real' representation of the subject captured. Unlike a drawing, photographs *generally* cannot be used to determine spatial relationships between objects—not at least without a specific intention to do so and only thereafter through careful preparations and execution of complementary methodologies to facilitate this intention at the time of acquisition (cf. immediately below)—nor do they disseminate *specific* archaeological interpretations. In summary, photographs must not be viewed as having supplanted drawings;

rather, both mediums are equally important in that they show different manners of looking at the surfaces of the archaeology. Therefore, as Barker (1993: 181) states, photographs function in a role that increases the archaeological understanding of a site by complimenting the drawn record.

Of course, the development of photography within the excavation has not simply remained only as a means to supplement archaeological drawings. Several applications have since been realised, but perhaps one of the more influential has been the application of photogrammetry within archaeology. Photogrammetry is a technique where accurate metric and semantic information is generated from photographs (Remondino 2014: 65). This technique is powerful because it enables an individual to reconstruct with photographs the spatial positioning, orientation, shape, and size of objects without having to be physically present in front of it (Kraus 2007: 1-2). In effect, this allows for the generation of 3D data from a 2D data source (Kraus 2007: 1; Remondino 2014: 65). The first true archaeological application of this technique occurred in 1956 when archaeologists were conducting a townscape study of an Italian town (Campana 2014: 9), although photogrammetric techniques may have been applied in archaeology as early as 1885 (Fussell 1982: 157). Regardless, since the mid-20th century, this application for photography has been conducted within archaeology to produce maps (Fussell 1982) and to facilitate the production of measured drawings (Cummer 1974; Fussell 1982; Nylén 1978)—especially those characterised by complex features (Jauregui and Jauregui 2000) and/or complex artefacts (Lagerqvist and Rosvall 2003).

Considering that photogrammetry allows photographs to be used as geometric references, there might be a reaction to view photogrammetry as a replacement for geometric archaeological drawings. However, there are limitations with photogrammetry that must be made explicit. Photogrammetry of course relies upon photographs, and as discussed previously, photographs function as an indiscriminate survey of the site. Photogrammetry naturally shares many of the same limitations that photography does. Thus, even though photogrammetry offers archaeologists the opportunity to conduct spatial analysis, this technique does not replace, but instead complements other forms of archaeological documentation.

The next significant technological leap within archaeology came with the increased computerisation of technologies within archaeology. The development of computer systems in turn lead to some traditional technologies getting an overhaul. For example, in the 1980s, the theodolite was used as the foundation for the development of the electronic distance measurement (EDM) total station (Drewitt 2011: 64). Designed as a device for surveying and producing topographical maps, total stations measure distances, angles, and elevations by describing these values as spatial coordinates relative to the total station itself (Nikon Corporation 2008). While archaeologists have utilised this technology in this very role, they have also applied it as a means to measure the elevation of archaeological units, to document the spatial location of artefacts, and to even 'trace' the limits of trenches and archaeological features. The major limitation of this technology is that it requires a computer to visualise the data that it produces. In fact, when one considers all of the technologies and their associated data discussed up to this point, it becomes quite apparent that they are all disjointed in relation to one another. Each represents different manners of focusing on the same material. Yet as relevant as these different perspectives are, by design they must also be presented as individual typologies apart from one another. What was needed was a way to tie these data—both spatial and non-spatial—together within one platform. The solution would be found in the geographic information system (GIS).

GIS has been a revolutionary technology for archaeology. A GIS refers to a suite of software where the chief application is as a database allowing for the storage and management of spatial information (Chapman 2009: 14). Thus, archaeologists have moved away from paper databases and embraced the efficiency offered by computerised (GIS) databases (Wescott 2005: 1). Secondarily, and dependent on the efficiency of the first, GISs are capable to transcend the storage and management of data to include the ability to manipulate, analyse, and visualise data (Chapman 2009: 15). Such properties intrinsic to GIS allow the user a new manner with which to interact and ultimately understand spatial information (Conolly and Lake 2006: 11).

Upon their first development, GISs were limited only to one of two typologies of digital data—raster or vector (Chapman 2009: 15). Today, however, most GISs are capable of working with both types of data. What is evident regarding GIS is that, when used correctly, it represents an incredibly powerful and diverse tool, which is capable of the absolutely crucial process of managing multiple typologies of data in logical and consistent manners, to more complex and technical operations involved with the analysis of those data (Conolly and Lake 2006: 10). There is little doubt that GIS has affected the whole of archaeology (Chapman 2009: 9; Lucas 2001: 128; for a list of broad applications within archaeology cf. Wescott and Brandon 2005).

More importantly for this work is the impact that GIS has had within field archaeology; it can be stated confidently that the implications have been profound. Field archaeology has traditionally been divided into tasks to be accomplished *during* the excavation and also *after* the excavation (what is commonly referred to as 'post-excavation') (Conolly and Lake 2006: 36; cf. also chapter divisions in Drewitt 2011). The large datasets pulled from the process of excavation necessitated a specific and undivided attention to detail that was not feasible during field investigations; thus, there was a natural division between the two. Furthermore, the introduction of computers and the subsequent digitisation of technologies resulted both in an enlargement of data within datasets and also a generation of entirely new typologies of data altogether. Of course, computer storage and processing technology progressed forward with the result being the development of more compact and mobile computers. Such leaps in technology saw the movement of the computer from the office and/or lab into the field itself—thereby causing the dividing lines between excavation and post-excavation duties to become blurred. The combined field operation of a total station alongside of a GIS platform illustrates the closing of this gap: spatial data gathered by the total station can be immediately input into the excavation GIS. This allows for the spatial data to become processed, stored, and linked with other archaeological data within the same GIS at the time of acquisition (Conolly and Lake 2006: 36-37). This is only one example of a typology of data that can be managed by GIS in the field. More recently, there has been a trend to take 3D models and place these beside other typologies of data within a GIS. This effectively results in a 3D GIS—the development of which absolutely lends credibility to the prediction that GIS may be "destined to have as profound an effect on the field of archaeology as did the introduction of carbon dating in the 1950s" (Wescott 2005: 1).

In order to understand why a 3D GIS is so impacting for field archaeology, it must first be defined what 3D models actually are. The concept of 3D models refers to a type of data by which the 'real' world and its three-dimensional properties are translated into computerised representations via mathematics that simulate those three-dimensional properties (Szeliski 2011: 3). While 3D models are most widely recognised for their entertainment value, these models also hold many benefits for scientific endeavours. However, for a 3D model to be recognised as scientifically valuable, it must have a well-defined purpose oriented towards answering specific questions or providing specific data (Hermon and Nikodem 2008: 1-2). Thus, bearing this in mind, 3D models must help archaeologists document in manners unachievable before. Traditionally, the only way to document archaeological objects was to translate their real-world 3D properties into 2D representations (e.g. through graphical mediums like drawings and photographs). With the introduction of 3D models, however, archaeologists were given the opportunity to document archaeological objects as they are found *in situ*—as three-dimensional entities (Campana 2014: 7). The development of 3D models can be accomplished through different technologies. For field archaeology, two technologies stand out as the most common: laser scanners and multi-view stereo reconstruction techniques (MSR).

Laser scanners refer to a group of technologies that produce dense point clouds or polygon meshes by measuring the real-world through lasers, lights, or x-rays (3D Systems 2014) and come in two primary types, laser triangulation and time-of-flight scanners. Both utilise different methods of laser measurement and thus have different applications. Laser triangulation scanners are designed for short-range applications and function by systematically moving a laser beam (focused into either a point or line) across the surface of an object. The distance and angles between the laser source and receiving sensor are precisely known, thus the sensor determines the distance of the object's surface through trigonometric triangulation by measuring the angle that the light is reflected back towards the scanner (3D Systems 2014; Guidi 2014: 39-42). The other typology of scanners, time-of-flight laser scanners, excel in mid- to long-range applications and function by measuring the amount of time it takes the laser to fire, reflect off the object, and return to the scanner. The laser emitter and receiving sensor are afforded a 360-degree view around itself by either moving these components directly or aiming the beams via a mirror (Al-kheder et al. 2009: 540; 3D Systems 2014; Guidi 2014: 42-44). In field archaeology, laser scanners offer archaeologists the ability to describe the entirety of their site as very high-quality 3D dense point clouds. Such applications for laser scanners have been hailed as providing a means for preserving (representations of) archaeological material (Al-kheder et al. 2009; Balzani et al. 2004); disseminating archaeological data as representations amongst specialists (Al-kheder et al. 2009; Balzani et al. 2004; Guidi 2014); production of orthophotos (Bennett 2011: 21-22; Davies 2011: 37-38); production of detailed sections and plans of highly complex features (Clarke 2011: 25-26); and recording the stratigraphy exposed over the course of an excavation (Doneus and Neubauer 2005).

The second technology involved with the development of 3D models within the field setting is MSR. This technique relies upon a dataset made up of overlapping photographs. These photographs are input within a software which first searches for shared points between photographs, then aligns those points, and through mathematical algorithms, utilises those points to develop a 3D representational model of the subject(s) captured (Szeliski 2011: 3). Since MSR depends on photographic datasets to create the models, the least-complicated choice for data collection is therefore digital JPG images—a format of image that allows the ability to quickly capture and produce ready-to-view images that can be uploaded directly from the camera to the computer without the need for photographic development processes. For field archaeology, there is an important distinction that must be made regarding MSR and other 3D documentation techniques. Unlike laser scanners and photogrammetry, which can be costly and time-consuming endeavours (Forte et al. 2012), MSR is considerably low-cost and time-saving in comparison—a fact that is attestable through experiments proving MSR to be capable of functioning within the time-span of the excavation where it can be used to produce daily 3D models of entire excavation sites and trenches (Dellepiane et al. 2013; also Forte et al. 2012). Furthermore, MSR techniques are inherently easier to transport compared to laser scanners in that they rely upon the humble digital camera which can easily be carried in a hip bag. The laser scanner itself is considerably more heavy and bulky in comparison and requires a heavy tripod to stabilise it in order to effectively capture the subject.

MSR is still relatively new to archaeology; as such, some researchers have concerned themselves with the development of methodologies for general field documentation (Muzzupappa et al. 2013) and for specific use within the excavation process (Callieri et al. 2011; De Reu et al. 2014; Dellepiane et al. 2013). Others have focused more on specific applications for MSR including 3D modelling as supplemental to traditional documentation technologies (Koutsoudis et al. 2014); as a means to encourage dissemination of excavation data (Opitz et al. 2013); as a solution to facilitate the speed through which representations can be produced for presentation purposes (Ducke et al. 2011); a method of 'realistic' documentation for the preservation of endangered archaeological evidence (Fux et al. 2009); and production of orthophotos and maps (Verhoeven et al. 2012). More recent trends have seen the utilisation of MSR with the aim to create new systems for acquiring and visualising the excavation process and site itself. Some specific examples of these are explored in greater detail in the case study section later in this work.

As with all of the other technologies explored through this state of the art, it must be stressed that 3D models are not a replacement for traditional technologies. 3D models represent a unique perspective of archaeological information that, when combined alongside other documentation formats (especially together within a GIS), serve to aid our comprehension and interpretation of the material uncovered through archaeological investigation.

3 – Theory

"Archaeology is concerned with telling the story of the past and telling stories about the past".
E. B. W. Zubrow (2006: 8).

The development of such archaeological narratives rests within the realm of theory in that it provides a means for archaeologists to comment on evidence of prehistoric/historic events captured in the archaeological record (Darvill 2009). In other words, theory functions as the lens through which we develop a pipeline for investigation. This begins with the development of specific questions, leading into the application of methodologies designed to uncover evidence, and ending towards answering those questions through the organisation and interpretation of that data (and, frequently, the creation of new questions). This process should ideally result in the production of an archaeological report, scientific articles, and, potentially, also a popular science description. Thus, through these stages a logical conclusion is developed resulting from a discourse focused upon the archaeological material and experiences, and is presented to interested parties as a form of narrative—or more simply put, an archaeological *story*.

Technology is inescapably bound in partnership to theoretical perspectives; a fact that can be seen throughout the sciences. For example, the telescope had huge impacts upon how astronomers viewed the stars and our own position within the universe. The microscope, which captured the attention of other scientists such as biologists, allowed and enabled these scientists to view a world that is simply too small for the naked eye to see. Telescopes and microscopes—technology—have thus opened new data for us to analyse and interpret new ways of explaining things. Archaeologists are familiar with this progression as well. The trowel, as described above, has forced archaeologists to excavate slowly, methodically, and *thoughtfully*. Through the trowel we are capable of sensing—and furthermore interpreting—so much more detail. Therefore, it can be firmly stated that technology is capable of affecting theory as well as being an implement of it. It enables more specific and technically demanding questions and/or surveys (Zubrow 2006: 13-14, cf. especially *Table 1.1* on page 14), but at the same time (if the technology itself is limited or even if it does not yet exist), it may function to hinder and/or reduce some manners of thinking to mere foresights and dreams (Zubrow 2006: 13). The prominent question then becomes *what precise role does technology play within archaeology?*

This particular debate is perhaps most widely recognisable regarding the role of GIS in geography (cf. Wright et al. 1997), although it is also mirrored within archaeology—most notably regarding the archaeological role of GIS (cf. Conolly and Lake 2006), but also in relation to digital technologies in general (cf. Zubrow 2006). Two distinct and conflicting camps have risen from these discussions: one that sees digital technologies as 'science'; and the other that views digital technologies relegated as simple 'tools' (Conolly and Lake 2006: 3; Wright et al. 1997: 346-347; Zubrow 2006: 9).

As a science, 3D digital documentation technologies are understood as *active*, consequential, influential, and provoking. They command an ability to affect not only how we interpret data, but how we approach problems and ask questions. In a certain sense, digital technologies may be summarised as a lens through which we can view archaeology and pose questions about it. Advocates of this camp would therefore argue that these technologies are *theory-active* within general archaeological theory. They may also have so much power that they can influence their own unique theoretical perspectives (Zubrow 2006: 9). As such, digital technologies as a science bring with them their own unique set of problems that may cooperate or clash with other theoretical paradigms used in archaeology. In this role, GIS transcends disciplines such as geography and archaeology and becomes a discipline in its own right. As a science, GIS would necessitate the creation and mastery of a complete set of theories in order to locate its position as an academic discipline itself, rather than as a small component utilised by individual disciplines (Wright et al. 1997: 347).

On the other hand, digital technologies as a 'tool' are viewed as *inactive*—neutral elements relegated to the role of implements to be deployed and conducted by theory. They are tools, much like the trowel and camera, in that they are utilised in the production, management, and presentation of data (data that can is to be analysed and interpreted by archaeological theory). In this role, they require not necessarily the development of mastery but rather the *development of technical competence* (Wright et al. 1997: 347). As tools, digital technologies function as hands-on devices and are therefore viewed as *theory-inactive*. It is within the latter of these two camps that most research tied to technology within archaeology is focused. However, it has been emphasised that digital technologies are absolutely capable of functioning in both capacities—they command enough power to affect theory while at the same time enabling the performance of methodology (Zubrow 2006: 16; 22). What is perhaps more important to highlight regarding digital technologies and field archaeology is that "digital archaeologists create problems that require digital solutions" (Zubrow 2006: 12). In other words, digital technologies are capable of producing new forms of data—data that will (at the very least) demand some degree of alteration in current, if not altogether entirely new, theoretical frameworks for understanding these data.

Thus, in theme with this work, a specific group of technologies holds considerable relevance: *3D digital documentation technologies*. Archaeology is naturally involved with three dimensional space. However, until recently, archaeologists have had to record and visualise (with a few intriguing exceptions, cf.: Nordbladh 2012: 245-250 for an example of physical 3D models and miniatures, especially *Fig. 2* on page 248; and page 250 for an example of a 3D model from 1817 detailing the 3D aspects of a burial mound with novel uses of 2D materials) in manners that are inherently restricted to two dimensions because of the limitations in technology—e.g. most obviously, *paper*. Thus, plan/section drawings, artefact/monument drawings, maps, and photographs are all representations of 3D archaeological entities described upon a 2D surface (with 3D being described as having volume and/or having x, y, and z coordinates, and 2D as limited to being represented by only two coordinates x and y) (Campana 2014: 7). With the introduction of computers, the digitisation of older technologies, and the progressive development of newer digital technologies, archaeologists now have access to hardware and software that not only enables the recording of three dimensional data in high-resolution representations of the excavation, but the manipulation, analysis, interpretation, annotation, and visualisation of three dimensional archaeological representations as well. Thus, Zubrow's call for digital solutions for digital problems is irrefutably applicable in modern world archaeology and may be further honed by stating that *3D problems require 3D solutions*.

Another important theoretical perspective that is relevant to this discussion is that of reflexivity towards methodology. While most archaeologists would agree that archaeological data and archaeological 'facts' are inherently loaded with theoretical perspectives, fewer are willing to discuss the degree to which archaeological *practice* itself is laden with theory (Hodder 1999: 80). The practice of archaeology, Hodder argues, is intimately bound together with archaeological theory because it chiefly involves interpretation (1999: 81-82). This particular point is well summarised by Hodder through his statement that the act of archaeological interpretation begins immediately along the trowel's edge (Hodder 1999: 83). In other words, archaeologists are engaging in interpretation the moment that hand and trowel begin to explore the subtle and not-so-subtle variations present in the excavation surface—e.g. interpretations are made when the archaeologist decides which variations in texture or colour should be ignored or followed (Hodder 1999: 92). However, some aspects of archaeology require a fixed system of defining objects and contexts. Hodder points out that after a soil layer has been excavated, the opportunity to interpret it further, as it was *in situ,* has been lost—the resulting interpretation cannot be changed because that layer cannot be re-measured, re-analysed, or re-explored as is possible with an artefact (Hodder 1999: 93). Furthermore, archaeology needs fixed definitions so that there is something to compare and contrast archaeological entities against (Hodder 1999: 93). What is therefore required, Hodder states, is a methodology that is capable of fluidity between objects, contexts, and interpretations—especially within the process of excavation. In this manner, interpretation can be used to settle upon excavation and acquisition strategies.

All of this is applicable to digital technologies in that the archaeologist must make decisions based on the knowledge of the site and what needs to be done in order to select the appropriate tools and methodologies for the job.

Finally, a reflexive perspective on methodology enables multivocality—an important aspect that advocates for as many 'voices' to be heard and recognised in order to increase the shared understanding of something such as the archaeology uncovered through excavations. Hodder notes that this has been accomplished on a larger scale by the adoption of the single context method developed by the Museum of London Archaeological Service (1999: 93). This is a significant development for Hodder because it took the right of interpretation away from the site director and placed it within the hands of the excavators themselves. In other words, because the single context method required each individual to record her/his own interpretation of the site, the excavators were thus encouraged to participate in the narration of the archaeology discovered (Hodder 1999: 93-96). Whereas such a process has been usually undertaken through traditional methodologies, newer digital technologies promise these individuals even more opportunities to document and share their interpretations regarding the archaeology that they have experienced.

Therefore, theory today, especially in regards to the relationship between the current state of the art of technology and archaeological excavation, can be boiled down to a simple yet important role: theory defines what technologies are selected and how those technologies are used. Not only is each site itself different, but there will always be variations in the amount of resources available (e.g. especially time and money) as well as variations with what technologies (and individuals with the training and skill to use those technologies) are available. Theory can then be utilised as guidance towards the selection of the best technology that will enable the collection of the most accurate and useful information with the amount of available resources.

4 – Methodology

To demonstrate how the current state of the art and theory are applied in practice, a few examples have been described in the pages following. These examples have been selected because they stand as testament to how digital technologies have been applied within archaeology and are thus central to the theme that has been explored in this work.

4.1 – Review of Established Methodologies and Associated Technologies

The first example is represented by work conducted by Callieri et al. (2011) who analysed the impact that dense stereo reconstruction tools might have for archaeologists when used in the field during the excavation itself. The experiments were conducted during the course of excavations in the 2011 season as part of the Uppåkra Research Project (Sweden). The researchers were interested in demonstrating novel applications of 3D modelling during the excavation process. Other modelling technologies, such as laser scanners, were noted to be too expensive and time consuming for use within an excavation. Dense stereo reconstruction, a considerably less-expensive and less-time consuming process of 3D modelling, was therefore selected to demonstrate the role 3D modelling could play in the excavation setting (Callieri et al. 2011).

The researchers first developed a complete pipeline from data acquisition (to model creation) through to model visualisation. This pipeline was aimed at providing a logical and user-friendly methodology that could be applied within an excavation after only a brief amount of instruction. In order to exemplify the process, the researchers employed the archaeologists working on excavating the site to demonstrate the feasibility of such a pipeline. To demonstrate the benefits of this pipeline outside of user-competence, the researchers also ensured that one model of the site was produced daily in order to document the site. The reason behind this was to demonstrate the technology's ability to be layered upon one another in order to produce a chronological record of the excavation process in 3D. Furthermore, these models were also shown to function in a variety of archaeological studies. For example, such functions of the models include: the measurements of archaeological surfaces; the inspection of geometry through selectively alternating between shaders/unique angles of lighting; the production of snapshots showing difficult (archaeologically relevant) perspectives of the excavation; and the ability to instantaneously rotate through a variety of perspectives with ease (Callieri et al. 2011).

Of significant relevance is the demonstration that 3D models can be used by the archaeologists to annotate directly upon the 3D models with archaeologically relevant information—thereby creating a fusion of 'real' representation as provided by the photo-realistic texture upon the 3D model, and specialist drawings that highlight what the archaeologist perceives as features of particular archaeological relevance. This case study clearly demonstrates that 3D models can be used alongside other traditional methodologies. It is also able to show that 3D models have novel applications that set them apart from those that have been utilised traditionally by archaeologists.

A second example of the importance of 3D digital models can be seen through the *Gabii Goes Digital* project (cf. Opitz et al. 2013). The project was realised in order to address a growing need to publish and share vast quantities of non-traditional (digital) data. Through their work, the Gabii Goes Digital team is able to present how 3D digital models are important for establishing a transparency of methodologies and interpretations, while also functioning as an important tool for the dissemination of archaeological knowledge to a wide audience of archaeological and non-archaeological spectators. The central documentation technology for their work at Gabii has been 3D models produced through MSR. Opitz et al. (2013) note that these models allow for a wide array of archaeological knowledge to be disseminated amongst specialists and the public alike. The problem they have identified is that, despite the number of projects experimenting with techniques like MSR, there has been little effort spent in establishing how these models can be efficiently shared, integrated into publications, visualised, and archived (Opitz et al. 2013). Their answer to these issues is to bring 3D digital models out from the appendix and into the core of archaeological work. In this manner they argue that it forces these models to become more visible and—most importantly—scrutinised in the peer-review process.

The Gabii Goes Digital team produces and disseminates their digital documentation data through a specific pipeline that includes five steps: 1) the collection of photographic and geospatial points; 2) the production of 3D models through Photoscan and the development of a database; 3) the construction of scenes using the 3D digital models—this environment also allows for the visualisation of the models and for the testing of theories; 4) encouragement of interactivity by linking the models together with other sources of information; and 5) the development of stratigraphic sequences. These data are all contained within a web-based database and are viewable (in limited format) to anyone with access to the internet. Using this workflow in conjunction with the visualisation medium, Opitz et al. are able to interrogate 3D digital archaeological data in a manner that encourages it to be peer-reviewed. Their process brings clarity to the decisions made during the excavation itself and during the interpretation using the 3D models—transparency is achieved—which in turn allows for these 3D digital data to come under analysis by other researchers. Finally, the medium itself is a useful way to engage public interest and share specialised archaeological knowledge.

The work produced by De Rue et al. (2014) offers a third example of methodologies exploring these technologies. De Rue et al. boldly state that MSR 3D digital models hold the potential to revolutionise archaeological excavation practice (2014: 261). They support this statement by demonstrating a multitude of applications that 3D models can fulfil: these models allow for archaeologists to transcend the two-dimensional recording mediums in favour of mediums involving three-dimensions. Such progress, De Rue et al. argue, secures the ability to understand the site more fully in the present and in the future (De Rue et al. 2014: 251). In their work, De Rue et al. set forth to take the next logical step in for methodologies concerned with MSR through introducing MSR as a technique for recording on a larger, excavation-wide scale.

To accomplish their goal, De Rue et al. utilised MSR in place of traditional methodologies that would have been used to record excavation surfaces, stratigraphy, sections, profiles, and samples (De Rue et al. 2014: 252). The models were made using Photoscan and were produced immediately after recording. In place of plan drawings, orthophotos were derived from the models; to provide the concept of height, DSM (Digital Surface Models) were used as an accompaniment (De Rue et al. 2014: 254). All models were located within both a 2D and 3D GIS to allow for their integration into the archaeological excavation database. Shapefiles were linked to the aforementioned orthophotos and contained information such as context numbers, descriptions, and interpretations (De Rue et al. 2014: 254). Vertically oriented orthphotos were used to capture stratigraphic data (De Rue et al. 2014: 256-259). In some instances, these section views were used to produce digital section drawings and, when combined with the orthophotos and DSMs, used for archaeological plan drawings—thus, the full range of archaeological documentation was achieved (De Rue et al. 2014: 259).

What De Rue et al. concluded was that 3D digital models, produced through MSR, promoted a significant increase in the overall quality of recording in comparison to traditional methods (De Rue et al. 2014: 260). Furthermore, they stated that the 3D models facilitated the further understanding of the archaeological data as it was recorded as it existed: in *three dimensions*. The last important result stated was that 3D models, when combined with other forms of archaeological documentation data, almost allow for an archaeologist to virtually revisit certain phases of the excavation. In summary, they concluded that the scientific quality presented by the use of 3D digital models surpasses anything that can be produced through traditional methodologies (De Rue et al. 2014: 262).

In a fourth and final example, Dell'Unto in his article (cf. Dell'Unto 2014) discusses the role of 3D models within the excavation process. He expressly focuses on exploring how 3D models and traditional data can be utilised together throughout an excavation, defining the relevancy of 3D models as geometrical references for the documentation of site features, and whether the application of novel visualisation technologies aid in comprehension of the stratigraphy throughout the investigation process itself (Dell'Unto 2014: 153). As with the first example, this one too was conducted within excavations at Uppåkra. In order to produce the 3D models necessary, Dell'Unto opted to utilise computer vision via digital photography (Dell'Unto 2014: 153). The data for this case study were acquired daily, resulting in a series of related 3D models that together documented the progression of the excavation (Dell'Unto 2014: 156). The 3D models were stored and visualised within ArcScene (Dell'Unto 2014: 156-157).

The 3D models were seen to function in a similar manner as traditional documentation methods in that they could be used to discuss the horizontal relationship between features and the development of the vertical stratigraphy (Dell'Unto 2014: 156). However, the 3D models also afforded viewpoints that were otherwise impossible with traditional methods of documentation—primarily because the 3D models enabled novel perspectives impossible to achieve in real-life (e.g. the ability to view in 3D, and in rapid succession, the chronological sequence of the excavation) (Dell'Unto 2014: 156). These unique applications of 3D models were noted to enhance the overall final interpretation of the site through a heightened awareness afforded by the three-dimensional representation of the site (Dell'Unto 2014: 156). Potential prospects were also demonstrated for the inclusion of these 3D models into the GIS used by the excavation (Dell'Unto 2014: 156-157). Dell'Unto also provides a description of how to accomplish such a 3D GIS—of special note is that ArcScene limits the number of polygons and textures for each 3D model imported (2014: 157).

In summary, Dell'Unto was able to demonstrate that 3D models have a definite place within the excavation process—one that does not replace traditional methodologies and technologies, but instead functions neatly within current excavation methodologies and complements documentation provided by traditional technologies. 3D models are thus demonstrated as representing a viable and impacting tool for use in the collection and visualisation of data in the excavation process.

4.2 – Introduction to Utilised Technologies

The methodology discussed in this work aimed to explore beyond the aspects presented above in order to analyse some of the limits and potentials that are offered by these technologies. In order to begin, it was necessary to harness the methodologies as described by Callieri et al. (2011), Opitz (2013), De Rue et al. (2014), and Dell'Unto (2014), to acquire the digital photography data for the experiment contained in this work. These data were used as source material for multi-view stereo reconstruction software in order to produce 3D models with photorealistic textures. The inclusion of geospatial reference points along the borders of the subject of acquisition have enabled the models to be georeferenced through use of a total station. The subsequent georeferenced models have then been input into a GIS, as described by Dell'Unto (2014), in order to establish a chronological sequence documenting the process of excavation surrounding one specific trench.

Beyond these previously established methodologies, however, this work has endeavoured to demonstrate how a more specific use of 3D polylines and polygons (to characterise the features detected during the archaeological investigation campaign), and the further customisation of the attribute tables intrinsic to GIS databases, may result in a more complete integration of the 3D models into the documentation system applied in the field. In order to maintain a continuity with traditional methodologies, all drawings have been accomplished in 3D upon the digital medium presented by GIS while grounding, as closely as possible, the 3D symbols to the original line symbols as set by the Museum of London Archaeological Service's single-context method of archaeological drawing (1994). Furthermore, both standard formats of archaeological drawing have been realised—e.g. plan and section drawings. In regards to the database component, every delineated archaeological feature has been allotted a unique context number. This identification number serves as a reference number for all relevant attributes—including those attributes typical of archaeological material as well as those that would normally be incorporated alongside of archaeological drawings—which have been input into the GIS database to allow for the potential to query for specific details. In short, the experiment developed aims to present that 3D models—in the framework of the archaeological excavation—can be utilised as geometrical references to (i) 'annotate' the information retrieved in the field and to (ii) use those information as a tool of discussion in the post-excavation phase.

A list of technologies, their descriptions, and how they have been applied within this work are provided immediately after the graphical depiction (FIGURE 4) below:

4.2.1 – Camera Systems

The photo acquisition campaigns for this work were accomplished using two DSLR (digital single-lens reflex) kits. The first kit was comprised of a Nikon D7000 camera body and a 10-24mm NIKKOR ultra-wide angle lens. The Nikon D7000 camera body is characterised by its high-quality DX CMOS APS-C 16.2-megapixel sensor that is capable of producing low-noise images in an ISO range between 100-6400. The letter combination 'DX' is used to denote a specific format of Nikon image sensors that conform to the Advanced Photo Systems standard of APS-C (or APS-Classic). This identifier describes the ratio size of the sensor which in this case is 3:2 (the traditional format of the average film camera). CMOS simply describes the type of integrated circuit used to build these sensors. It is useful to mention that the DX sensors have a crop factor of 1.5x, and as a result, the focal lengths of all lenses are effectively 'elongated' by 1.5x. In other words, a 10mm lens paired with a DX crop sensor will produce a photograph that would appear to be shot with a 15mm lens. It is beyond the scope of this work to go into a list of pros and cons regarding crop factors. However, it is pertinent to acknowledge that if one wants to utilise the full capabilities of a wide angle lens, it is most effective to employ a camera with an FX (full 35mm equivalent frame) sensor, where a 10mm lens will produce photographs characteristic of having been shot with a 10mm lens. A concise way of understanding crop factor is that it causes some of what the lens can 'see' (specifically the edges) to be omitted from the resulting image. Of course, this does not adversely affect the production of models, but instead may or may not make the acquisition campaign more difficult.

Two other notable features of this camera are that it is both rugged and weather-sealed—two characteristics that enable it to take a certain amount of punishment via the occupational hazards of dust, mud, and rain that are ever-present on an archaeological site (although such hazards should always be avoided if and whenever possible). One final important characteristic for this work is that the D7000 can simultaneously capture photographs in both JPG and RAW formats—the benefits of which allow the collection of high-quality, unadulterated raw photographic data for storage and production of superior-quality 3D models, while also facilitating the in-field production of models through the simultaneous creation of an identical lightweight and ready-to-use JPG image (which are an ideal format for usage with MSR techniques). Refer to Nikon Corporation (2014) (contained in section *9.2 Online Sources*) for a detailed list of specifications concerning the Nikon D7000 DSLR.

The lens utilised alongside of the Nikon D7000 in the first kit was a high-quality AF-S zoom 10-24mm f/3.5 - 4.5G ED NIKKOR ultra-wide angle lens that was specifically designed for use with DX format cameras (Nikon Corporation 2014a). This lens houses glass of a very good quality and is capable of producing incredibly sharp photographs. Owing to its ultra-wide focal length, however, there is a considerable amount of distortion that increases closer to the edges and corners of the photograph.

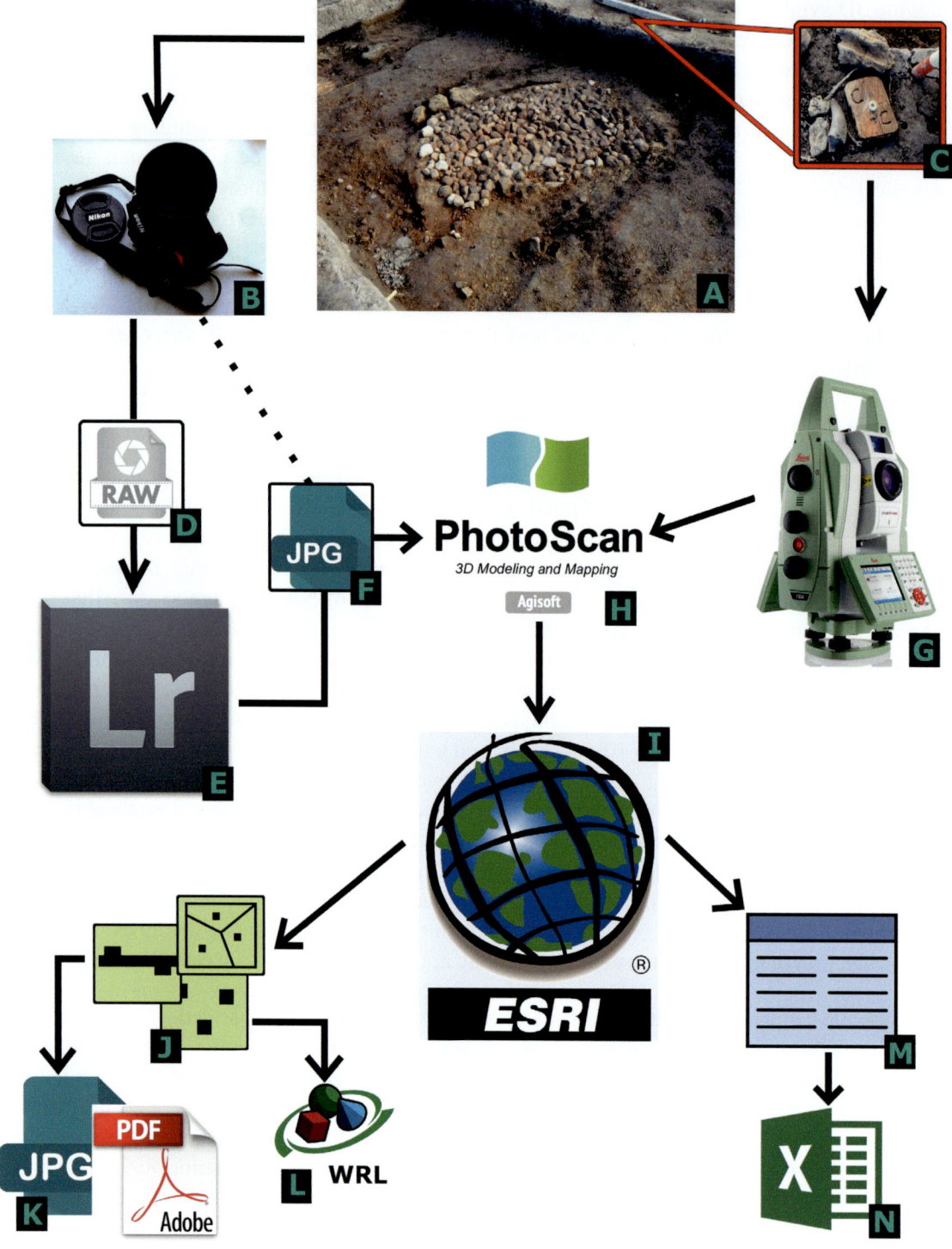

FIGURE 4 – A VISUAL DEPICTION OF THE PIPELINE OF TECHNOLOGIES USED IN THIS WORK'S EXPERIMENT. INCLUDED IN THE ABOVE LIST ARE THE FOLLOWING: (A) THE PHYSICAL ARCHAEOLOGICAL OBJECT; (B) DIGITAL SLR CAMERA; (C) CONTROL POINTS FOR GEOSPATIAL RECORDING; (D) RAW IMAGE FORMAT; (E) ADOBE PHOTOSHOP LIGHTROOM; (F) JPG IMAGE FORMAT; (G) EDM TOTAL STATION; (H) AGISOFT'S PHOTOSCAN; (I) ESRI'S 3D GIS ARCSCENE; (J) ESRI SHAPEFILES [POINTS, POLYLINES, AND POLYGONS]; (K) ARCSCENE 2D OUTPUT FORMATS [E.G. JPG AND PDF]; (L) ARCSCENE 3D OUTPUT FORMAT [E.G. WRL]; (M) ESRI ATTRIBUTE TABLES; AND (N) ARCSCENE TABLE OUTPUT FORMATS [E.G. MICROSOFT EXCEL]. (IMAGE BY J.J.L. KIMBALL 2014; ALL LOGOS AND ASSOCIATED CONCEPTS ARE COPYRIGHT OF THEIR RESPECTIVE COMPANIES).

The second kit consisted of a Canon EOS 550D camera body and a fixed focal length 15mm wide angle lens. Like its Nikon counterpart, the Canon EOS 550D also contains an APS-C CMOS sensor—however at 18 megapixels, the Canon sensor is slightly larger than the Nikon D7000 sensor. This sensor is also capable of producing low-noise images with a sensitivity range between 100 to 6400 ISO. The crop factor on the Canon 550D is slightly tighter than the Nikon at 1.6x (Canon Incorporated 2014). Thus, the 15mm lens used on this camera functions as if it were a 24mm wide angle lens. This camera was operated by Nicolo Dell'Unto (Lund University, Sweden), who was also acquiring 3D models of the excavations. Although I did not use this camera myself, it was important to recognise that some of the models used within this work were made with a camera system apart from my own. Refer to Canon Incorporated (2014) (contained in section *9.2 Online Sources*) for a detailed overview of the Canon EOS 550D.

It is of course necessary to stress that there are many other camera systems that are equal or better than the Nikon D7000 (as exemplified above); however, I have selected to use this specific camera in my work primarily because it was my own personal camera—a camera that I have selected as an upgrade in my personal kit to facilitate the production of high-quality photographs for my own professional photography business. There are other obvious rationales to such systems. Take as example the Nikon D7000 which, like its primary competitor the Canon EOS 60D, is a high-end consumer/semi-professional grade camera (also referred to as 'prosumer'). When paired with a selection of lenses covering a range between wide-angle, human-eye focal length equivalent (~50mm), and macro, these camera systems are likely to be one of the most standard pieces of equipment in the field archaeologists' tool box. As such, this work discusses the applications of this type of camera for the production of multi-view stereo reconstruction 3D models simply because of their availability, their capability of producing crisp, clean, detailed photographs, and the ability to have complete control over necessary image settings.

4.2.2 – Adobe Photoshop Lightroom 5.4

Adobe's Photoshop Lightroom is a photo editing and photo management software bundled into one package. As such, it has all of the necessary features required to process, or 'develop', any photographs captured. Of greatest importance is that it allows for the opening of RAW format files (e.g. Nikon's NEF) that would otherwise require special software apart from what is locally installed on most computers. Lightroom also allows for batch editing (a term referring to the photo editing of an entire group—a 'batch'—of images rather than one image at a time), which expedites the process of editing, converting (when recorded in RAW format), and exporting image files for use with multi-view stereo reconstruction 3D modelling software. Significantly, any modifications made to the images through Lightroom's editing software *do not alter the original file*. Instead, all changes made to the photographs are saved within Lightroom's catalogue (a photograph database system) as a metadata tag that describes the modifications and information data belonging to a specific RAW photograph. This is a particularly important characteristic to have at one's disposal as it allows for the raw data to be utilised on the spot when needed—but also allows for that same data to be stored in its original format for use when new developments in the technology come to pass in the future. At the rate that technology is evolving, it is very likely that new developments will improve the quality of the end product derived through techniques such as MSR. Thus it is critical to maintain a best-quality standard of data in order to ensure that such future possibilities can exploit the data of today (which remains as the only record of excavated features). Refer to Adobe Systems Incorporated (2014) (contained in section *9.2 Online Sources*) for a detailed explanation of Lightroom's features.

In summary, this software was selected primarily because it enables the storage and full control over the raw, unadulterated photographic data, thereby allowing for the archaeologist to export the necessary quality and resolution of the photograph for whatever application is required.

3D Delineation

4.2.3 – Agisoft's Photoscan 1.0.4

Agisoft's Photoscan is a standalone (does not require an internet connection) multi-view stereo reconstruction software. This software ranges in price from $180 for the standard edition to $3500 for the professional edition. While both produce the same quality of 3D models, the professional version allows for the model to be georeferenced in the software itself. The most difficult part of utilising this software is the production of usable photographs through a systematic process—everything else about the software is relatively straightforward. Photoscan, while operating best when used on more powerful desktop computers (e.g. Agisoft (2014), recommends that it be run on a desktop with an Intel Sandy Bridge 3930K processor, a motherboard with eight DDR3 slots and 1 PCI Express x16 slot, 64 GB of RAM (e.g. eight sticks of 8 GB DDR3 RAM), and an NVidia GeForce GTX 580 video card), can be run on laptop computers that have limited resources. For example, the laptop utilised for the production of models in this work (Intel Core i5 2.50 GHz processor, 8 GB of RAM, and an Intel Graphics video card with 1250 MB dedicated video memory [5300 MB with shared system memory]) has only a fraction of Agisoft's recommended computer specifications, yet it is still capable of producing high-quality 3D models. It must be emphasised that a less-powerful computer does not result in a lower quality model, but instead results in a longer processing time with a greater chance of failure (through the software freezing and/or crashing due to the limitations in computing power).

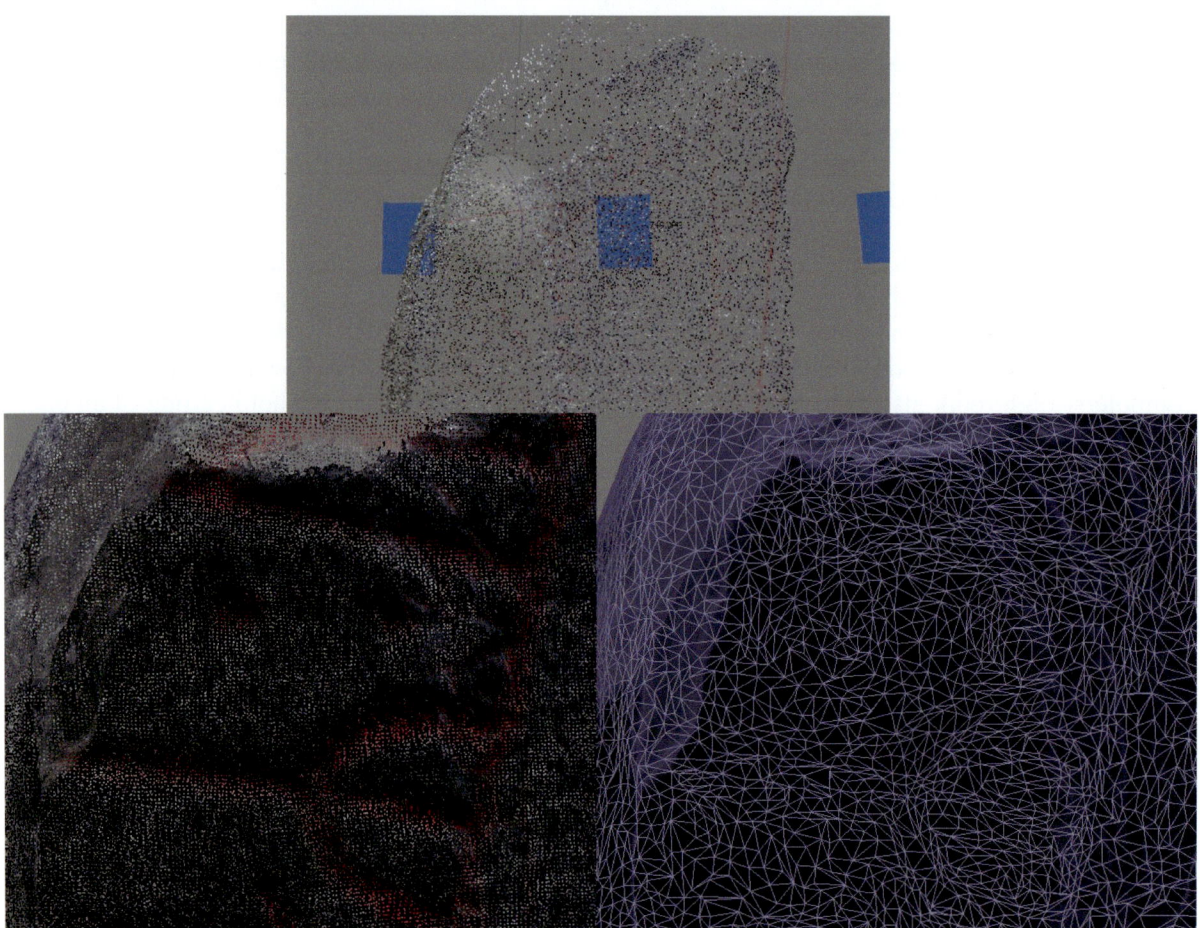

FIGURE 5 – (SCREEN-CAPTURES OF A 3D MODEL) STEPS IN MSR PRODUCTION WITH PHOTOSCAN; (TOP) ESTIMATION OF INTERNAL CAMERA PARAMETERS AND CAMERA PROJECTIONS; (LEFT) DENSE-POINT CLOUD; (RIGHT) MESH. (IMAGE BY J.J.L. KIMBALL 2014; 3D MODEL BY J.J.L. KIMBALL 2014).

FIGURE 6 – (SCREEN-CAPTURE OF A 3D MODEL) THE FINAL STAGE OF MSR—A PHOTOREALISTIC 3D MODEL OF THE RUNESTONE DR 330 "GÅRDSTÅNGASTENEN 2" LOCATED IN LUND, SWEDEN. (IMAGE BY J.J.L. KIMBALL 2014; 3D MODEL BY J.J.L. KIMBALL 2014).

While there are many other software capable of producing multi-view stereo reconstruction 3D models, only Photoscan stands apart as an all-in-one inclusive program. Verhoeven (2011) offers a detailed explanation of how Photoscan works to construct 3D models. Simplistically, the process begins by the user feeding uncalibrated, overlapping images into the software. Through mathematical algorithms, the software detects and then tracks how points move throughout the series of images. During this initial step, the lens distortion from the photographs are also removed by separate algorithms using information about the lens contained within the metadata of the photographs. It is worth mentioning that after this step, the original data—the digital photographs—have effectively been utilised to create three new data sets: (i) an interrelated set of points common to multiple photographs; (ii) the establishment of the spatial location for the camera, in relation to the object of acquisition, for each aligned image; and (iii) the internal parameters of the camera relating to focal length and its distortion effects (Verhoeven 2011: 68). After this initial data creation, the next step is the development of a dense point cloud based on the matched points established in the first step. This is then followed by the construction of a triangulated mesh and finally by the photo-realistic texturisation of the model (Verhoeven 2011: 68-70). An example of the various steps in the process can be seen in FIGURE 5 and FIGURE 6, and, additionally, the reader will find 3D examples of MSR models via the link in the footnote below.[2]

These attributes intrinsic to Photoscan offer several benefits to archaeologists. Most important is that, as an all-inclusive and stand-alone software, archaeologists do not have to jump between other software programs to accomplish a fully-developed 3D model. Furthermore, this software does not require an internet connection. These two facts alone make Photoscan an ideal candidate for application within the field. Another benefit is that the developers have made the process itself incredibly flexible. For example, in between stages of model creation, the user can enable and disable certain photographs in order to achieve the best representation of the object possible. This is especially important for archaeologists as the 'organised chaos' present at a site undergoing excavations may present challenges—especially regarding the end-result of the texturisation process. Beyond simply creating a model, Photoscan also allows for the user to perform cleaning tasks on the resulting model, decimate it, and export it in a variety of formats such as OBJ, DAE, and PDF. Exportation into PDF is extremely important as it is by far the simplest and most far-reaching format allowing for the dissemination of 3D models. In the case of OBJ and DAE, this allows for the user to import the model into different software programs, such as 3DS Max or Blender for the development of an 'explorable' virtual scene of the excavation. Furthermore, if the professional version of Photoscan is used, one can also select points upon the model to mark with georeferenced data (e.g. points obtained via a total station or GPS). Once georeferenced, these models can then be imported into the GIS which allows for the integration of the models directly alongside other archaeological datasets. It is because of these features that Photoscan has been selected as the software of choice for producing multi-view stereo reconstruction 3D models in this work.

4.2.4 – EDM Total Station

A Leica EDM total station and accompanying prism were necessary tools for the experiment in this work. This instrument was utilised to record the spatial locations of anchor points that were positioned around the perimeter of Trench 5. It was also important that these points were located close to the edge in order to ensure that they would be recorded in the photographs during the photo acquisition campaign. In turn, this meant that those points would also be present on the 3D models which thereby would allow for them to be georeferenced directly in Photoscan and, ultimately, would facilitate their accurate placement alongside of other spatial information within the GIS platform. Whereas a survey-grade GPS system could have also been used to gather these points, the excavation leaders favoured the use of an EDM total station for practically all spatial recording; as such, it was logical to also utilise this system because of its availability on site, and because of its use for the documentation of all other spatial data.

---

[2] For an example of a 3D model produced through MSR, cf. various media under the title "MSR Runestone" in the following webpage: https://sites.google.com/site/justinjlkimball/masters-data

4.2.5 – ArcGIS 10.2.1

The suite of software offered through ESRI's ArcGIS—particularly ArcMap—has been an industry standard in archaeological practice for quite some time. A basic definition of GIS would be that it allows for the storage, manipulation, analysis, query, and visualisation of spatial data (ESRI 2014; Chapman 2009: 15). It is important to recognise that while ArcMap does store three-dimensional data, the software is limited in that it must visualise the depth value of spatial data in graphical form on top of a two-dimensional plane. Such graphical representations have commonly been accomplished through the use of contour lines and spot heights (Chapman 2009: 43-44). However, through ArcScene, 3D spatial data can be visualised in a 3D digital environment. Furthermore, and most importantly, ArcScene allows for the visualisation of 3D spatial data in both raster and vector formats. As 3D models are constructed from both vector and raster data, they can be visualised within ArcScene. It must be stressed that, at least at the time of writing this, ESRI's ArcScene is the only software capable of performing these operations.

For archaeologists, this is an extremely important development. At the most basic level this software allows for 3D models to be included alongside of other spatial data. More importantly, however, is that the database functions intrinsic to ArcGIS can therefore be applied directly to these models. Furthermore, the user can utilise the editing capabilities of ArcScene to create new data, such as shapefiles, that are based specifically upon the 3D features of these models. These shapefiles can then be assigned specific attributes that are then also included within the database, thereby increasing the level to which these 3D models are integrated. In the end, this results in an increase in the relevancy that these models have towards both disseminating and generating archaeological knowledge.

4.3 – Limitations

There are some limitations regarding the methodology and selection of technologies discussed above that must be made explicit. First of all, the scope of focus was necessarily limited to a single trench within a single (and considerably brief) excavation. This limitation was imposed not just because of the short amount of time the excavation was conducted, but because of the limited amount of time given for the authoring of this work. By focusing specifically upon one sole trench, a high-quality, well-planned, and well-executed pipeline was created in the allotted time constraints. It was deemed to be more logical and effective to pursue the results in this manner so that an effective pipeline could be presented to future researchers for further testing such as determining its limitations when utilised on a project characterised by significantly greater complexity and size.

Another issue that should be highlighted is in reference to the selection of technologies. The pipeline developed is not meant to be restricted to using only these systems described above. A large factor in the selection of these technologies has resulted in what has been immediately and affordably available. Other researchers may have access to more or less of these technologies, but that in itself is not what should be understood as important. What instead must be recognised is that this pipeline should be viewed as a framework to which components can be added, removed, or replaced with others in order to facilitate both the technologies available to a field excavator and the scope of the research question being asked. For example, one could just as easily use a completely different camera system instead of the one used in this work; or, perhaps instead of using ArcGIS, one might try using another similar GIS platform when another is inevitably developed as a competitive response to ESRI's ArcScene. Yet, despite that this work was limited to available technologies, and others may indeed function as suitable replacements or additions, it must also be acknowledged that those tools listed previously work well together in the established pipeline and are therefore highly recommended. Perhaps an interesting future endeavour for research would be to explore other combinations of technologies in order to see what sorts of results might be produced.

5 – Experiment: 3D Delineation

The experiment described below demonstrates how 3D models may be further integrated into a GIS—a union that not only increases the relevance of 3D models as archaeological source material, but also leads to the creation of new forms of data that are of value for archaeological research. The data for the experiment were acquired during the 2013 autumn field excavations at Uppåkra, Sweden, while the process of 3D digital delineation was performed throughout the 2014 spring semester.

5.1 – General Background of Uppåkra

Managed today by Lund University, Uppåkra is a rich archaeological site located 5km south of the city of Lund in the province of Skåne, Sweden. First discovered in 1934, this unique cultural heritage site has been the focus of intensive archaeological investigation since the inception of the Uppåkra Research Project in 1996. A series of excavations in conjunction with field surveys and metal-detector surveys has revealed that Uppåkra was an extensive settlement site covering over 40 hectares of land. This size gives Uppåkra the distinction of being the largest known settlement site in southern Sweden (Larsson 2007: 12). Metal-detector surveys turned up nearly 20,000 finds that helped to date the site as ranging from the pre-Roman Iron Age through to the Viking Age. The majority of the metallic items were concentrated within an area located on top of the highest point of elevation within the settlement area (Larsson 2007: 12). Excavations in this area began in 1999 and between 2001 and 2005 a building of unusual construction—compared to others within the excavation area—was uncovered (Larsson 2007: 14). This building was found to contain an impressive number of gold-foil figures, a highly ornate silver and bronze beaker, and a glass bowl made from two layers of glass (Larsson 2007: 16). These factors have led researchers to consider this building to be of particular relevance, although there has been some disagreement on its function (e.g. whether it was a house, hall, or temple and whether the activities conducted there were of cult or ceremonial function) (Larsson 2007: 21).

In 2008, the focus shifted from the aforementioned and onto other buildings found within the settlement site: namely a series of large longhouses. The goal of these phase of investigation was to understand the chronological phases of those longhouses as well as their relationships to one another and the settlement site as a whole. (Söderberg and Piltz Williams 2012: 7). A geophysical survey conducted in the summer of 2010 through a partnership with the Ludwig Botzman Institute for Archaeological Prospection and Virtual Archaeology revealed a circular anomaly to the west of the Uppåkra churchyard (Dell'Unto 2014: 153-154; Söderberg and Piltz Williams 2012: 7; Trinks et al. 2013: 34). In 2011, two distinct excavations were pursued: the first, named Stora Uppåkra 8:3, focused at continuing the exploration of the longhouses that was started in 2008 (Söderberg and Piltz Williams 2012: 10-11) while the second, named Stora Uppåkra 8:4, was directed towards exploring the circular anomaly discovered by the geophysical survey (Söderberg and Piltz Williams 2012: 12).

The excavations at Stora Uppåkra 8:3 revealed that there was a connection between the longhouses visible in the modern excavations and those found in the 1934 excavations. Of the houses examined, house number 22, a longhouse from the Viking age, was noted to have two phases: a younger and an older. The older phase was defined entirely, while the younger phase was found to continue eastward beyond the limits of the excavation (Söderberg and Piltz Williams 2012: 7). The second excavation at Stora Uppåkra 8:4 was aimed at investigating whether there was a relationship between the anomaly and Iron Age graves. While the anomaly was a grave, it was revealed to be from the middle to late Neolithic rather than the Iron Age. While this did not answer any questions about Iron Age graves related to the Iron Age settlement at Uppåkra, it was exceptional nonetheless considering that graves of this style have not been previously documented in Skåne (Söderberg and Piltz Williams 2012: 7).

The most recent excavations at Uppåkra, in 2013, were conducted in the field to the west of the modern church (FIGURE 7) and were aimed at: (i) following up the results of the geophysical survey conducted in 2010; (ii) defining the purpose of the area: and (iii) determining whether that purpose was related to the craft industry at Uppåkra (Apel and Piltz Williams 2014, in press). The actual process of excavation was conducted by undergraduate and graduate students. In order to explore these goals, five trenches were made—each focusing on a different anomaly revealed by the geophysical survey. The archaeological investigation revealed the remains of buildings and paved surfaces, a historical road, cooking pits, and an oven (Apel and Piltz Williams 2014, in press). The archaeological stratigraphy at Uppåkra is characterised by many complex layers—a factor that attracts many researchers that become involved in experimenting with new techniques and methodologies. The excavations also present an ideal learning environment for students.

5.2 – Documentation Methodology at Uppåkra since 2011

All excavation surveys were documented following the single-context method. At Uppåkra, all layers, burials, features, and finds were measured in with an EDM Total Station and then stored and visualised within Riksantikvarieämbetet's *Intrasis*—a GIS platform. All archaeological objects were denoted by their stratigraphic relationships and provided with a unique number that was part of an ongoing sequence. Objects were also organised by their relational arrangement: youngest to oldest. All layers were geospatially documented and tied into the Lund municipality coordinate system. Student excavators were required to keep a dig diary that discussed their findings and interpretations for the day. These diaries were then used by the students to author reports covering the areas and contexts they were involved with.

FIGURE 7 – A PHOTOGRAPH LOOKING SOUTHWARD OVER TOP OF SEVERAL OF THE 2013 EXCAVATION TRENCHES. (PHOTOGRAPH © J.J.L. KIMBALL 2013).

Manual documentation in the form of archaeological plan and section drawings were done whenever it was deemed necessary to enrich the archaeological documentation of the site. Photographs were captured via digital camera and, in some instances, those photographs were taken with the purpose in mind to create 3D models (Apel and Piltz Williams 2014, in press; Söderberg et al. 2014: 11; Söderberg and Piltz Williams 2012: 12-13).

5.3 – State of the Art: 3D Modelling at Uppåkra

Through collaborative efforts between Lund University and the Visual Computing Lab in Pisa, experiments were developed to understand the advantages and disadvantages of 3D models as an excavation tool for documentation and interpretation (Dell'Unto 2014: 152-153). One of the first experiments was aimed at determining what technology (time-of-flight laser scanner vs. computer vision)[3] was best suited for use within an excavation setting. While laser scanners were found to be suitably efficient for acquiring 3D data from the site, the time and skill needed to post-process the data was unfeasible for the time constraints typical of field excavations (Dell'Unto 2014: 153). Computer vision on the other hand, was demonstrated to be a feasible technology for such application. One of the influential factors that set computer vision apart from laser scanning was the that latter simply relied upon the comparatively inexpensive, uncalibrated digital camera. Furthermore, the software needed to produce the models required relatively little experience apart from a general explanation of the system. Thus, the ease of acquisition and visualisation made computer vision software a strong contender for the intended applications under a limited time frame (Dellepiane et al. 2013: 209; Dell'Unto 2014: 153).

The first experiment at testing the viability of 3D models developed through computer vision software was attempted during the summer of 2010 on one of the longhouses undergoing excavation. The goals of the experiment were to determine the limitations of the technology with particular attention paid to the number of models the technology could produce in a short time frame and whether the quality of the models would be acceptable for archaeological use. It was demonstrated that computer vision was indeed able to produce models consistently alongside of the excavation in a time frame suitable for use during ongoing work and that those models were sufficiently accurate to be used as geometric references for documentation (Dell'Unto 2014: 153). The major limitation of this experiment was that the conducting team was not part of the excavation team. Thus they could not accurately comment on whether this technology was truly a sufficient tool for utilisation during an excavation campaign by the excavators themselves.

A second experiment was outlined and conducted during the 2011 summer excavation of the Neolithic grave (Stora Uppåkra 8:4). The goals of this experiment were to investigate the feasibility of a documentation methodology based on the combined use of 3D models and other traditional documentation technologies, to evaluate 3D models as geometrical references, and to determine whether 3D models could function to increase the understanding of the stratigraphic sequence over the course of the excavation process (Dell'Unto 2014: 153). In order to establish that this technology was applicable for regular use in field archaeology, the researchers demonstrated to the excavation archaeologists how to perform the acquisition and visualisation processes (Dell'Unto 2014: 156). What was found was that the 3D models provided archaeologists with perspectives that would have otherwise been difficult or impossible to achieve. It was concluded that 3D models aided in a deeper understanding of the site, especially concerning the stratigraphy, and helped to produce a richer interpretation of the archaeology (Dell'Unto 2014: 156). Although the researchers were unable to accomplish the goal of combining the 3D models with traditional data, they did determine that the absence of multi-tiered documentation results in a less-impacting role for 3D models in relevance to the documentation strategy as a whole (Dell'Unto 2014: 156).

---

[3] Over the last few years, MSR techniques have been referred to by several names including 'computer vision'. At the time of writing his 2014 article, Dell'Unto referred to the MSR technique as 'computer vision'.

A major methodological stride to come from this second experiment was concerned with visualisation solutions for 3D models—namely GIS. Endeavours made by the companies that produce GIS platform have recently acknowledged a need to incorporate the ability to manage and visualise 3D models in their software. The researchers took this opportunity and began the process of importing their 3D models into ESRI's ArcGIS. They relied upon Agisoft's Photoscan because of its ability to produce georeferenced models—allowing them to be positioned geographically within the GIS itself (Dell'Unto 2014: 156-157). The inclusion of these 3D models into the excavation GIS thus allows for the models to be incorporated alongside of other documentation types. Therefore, models are not only managed and visualised alongside other relevant information, they can also be given attributes and, through those attributes, become enabled as potential targets for querying (Dell'Unto 2014: 157).

5.4 – Experiment Overview

Uppåkra is a complex site—a particular characteristic that becomes especially apparent when looking at the many minute layers of stratigraphy. Other complexities also include a consideration to the number of individuals working at the site and the variety of research projects ongoing at any given time. Further compounding these issues are that excavations generally only last a few weeks at most, making the entire archaeological experience very short and truncated. It is bearing these factors in mind that the overarching goal of this experiment hopes to address with the established methodology. The framework for this work's methodology has been based upon those that are both well-established (e.g. archaeological drawing) and recently brought to light (e.g. the works by Callieri et al. 2011; Dellepiane et al. 2013; and Dell'Unto 2014).

While the documentation methods at Uppåkra are tried and true, they are not without their problems. Of most concern is that they can be time consuming, tedious, prone to operator-error, and are simply fixed in one perspective. This experiment therefore proposes a novel use for the employment of a GIS platform to not only visualise 3D models, but demonstrate that a 3D/4D GIS (3D referring of course to 3D data within a 3D GIS environment and 4D referring to the chronological sequencing or 'layering' of such data within the 3D GIS) can perform certain documentation tasks that have been considered as primarily belonging within the roles of traditional methodologies in archaeological documentation. As has been stated before: these techniques are not to be viewed as replacements for traditional documentation techniques. Instead, this experiment shows that these applications function to compliment traditional documentation methodologies when used alongside them and, furthermore, may offer a viable solution when traditional methodologies are not feasible because of constraining factors.

I have made an attempt to present this experiment in a manner that is conducive for all field applications, but I also recognise that my solutions may be heavily coloured by my own experiences at Uppåkra—a site that has its own unique problems that may or may not be relevant to other sites. However, I stand by my convictions that this experiment has demonstrated an important new documentation technique provided through the use of a 3D GIS.

5.5 – Experiment Methodology

The experiment developed for this work can be broken down into five distinct steps: 1) the creation of the 3D models through MSR; 2) the introduction of those 3D models into the excavation GIS to establish a 3D/4D GIS; 3) the actual drawing in 3D overtop of those models within the GIS itself; 4) the linking of those drawings into the GIS database; and 5) the visualisation and output of those models and drawings in various 2D and 3D formats. The first step, out of necessity, included the photographic acquisition campaign and was achieved during the 2013 autumn excavations at Uppåkra. Prior to any photographic documentation, a series of points were placed and recorded via total station around the trenches (FIGURE

FIGURE 8 – A PHOTOGRAPH FROM ONE OF THE ACQUISITION CAMPAIGNS AROUND TRENCH 5; NOTE THE MARKERS ALONG THE EDGES OF THE TRENCH. (PHOTOGRAPH © J.J.L. KIMBALL 2013).

8). The points collected were then stored within the excavation GIS and were later used to georeference the 3D models. Enough photographic data was captured to create six unique 3D models of four different trenches. Despite the capture of these four trenches, the experiment in this work focuses solely upon the 3D models of Trench 5. For my own acquisition campaign, my camera was set to capture RAW images to be later developed into high-quality JPG images. The methodology of the acquisition was done in the manner established by Callieri et al. (2011) for field archaeological applications where the operator must move around the target while taking a series of overlapping photographs. The photographs were uploaded from the camera's memory card to Adobe Photoshop's Lightroom software where the images were organised into specific folders representing individual and distinct datasets. It was within this software where the conversion from RAW to JPG was conducted. In order to render the data into 3D format, the datasets were input into Agisoft's Photoscan. When creating the models, the parameters were set to high-quality settings in order to produce incredibly detailed models. The texturisation process was also set to the highest quality in order to ensure the creation of high resolution, photorealistic textures. These models were stored in their own folders within their respective datasets.

The second step involved the importation of the 3D models into ESRI's ArcGIS. This was accomplished by following the methodology set forth by Dell'Unto (2014: 156-157) which results in the establishment of a 3D/4D GIS. It was first necessary to apply the geospatial data of each real-world anchor point (the data of which was acquired by the on-site total station) to its corresponding virtual-world anchor point (e.g. the point visible upon the 3D model itself). This task was accomplished directly within the professional version of Photoscan. The 3D models were then decimated in Photoscan to ensure that they would not exceed the maximum amount of polygons defined by ArcGIS. Thereafter, the decimated models were exported into a 3D file format readable by the ESRI's ArcGIS. When imported into ArcGIS, the software was able to recognise the geographical coordinates stored within the models. This made it possible for ArcGIS to automatically position each model within its appropriate geographical position in relation to the other data contained in the database (FIGURE 9).

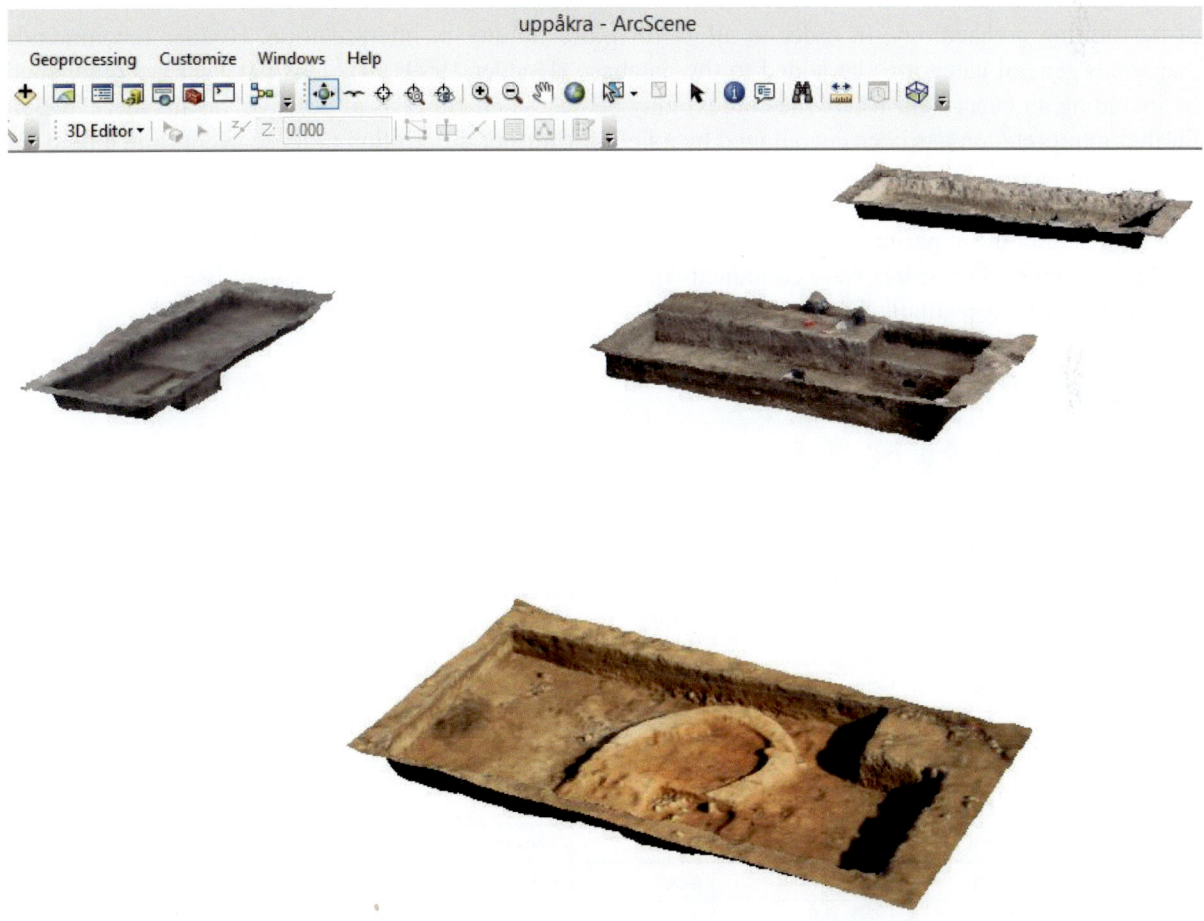

FIGURE 9 – (SCREEN-CAPTURE) THE 3D MODELS LOCATED WITHIN THEIR PROPER GEOSPATIAL LOCATIONS WITHIN ARCSCENE. (IMAGE BY J.J.L. KIMBALL 2014; 3D MODELS AND GIS IMPLEMENTATION BY N. DELL'UNTO AND THE DEPARTMENT OF ARCHAEOLOGY AND ANCIENT HISTORY, LUND UNIVERSITY 2013).

3D Delineation

Once the models were located inside of the GIS, the main portion of the experiment was set to take place marking the beginning of step three—the act of 3D drawing over top of 3D models within ArcScene. The drawings were enabled by the use of shapefiles (e.g. points, polylines, and polygons)—the properties of which are well known within the standard applications of GIS. The experiment aimed to replicate the line symbology for archaeological drawing as defined by the single-context method (Museum of London Archaeological Service 1994). ArcGIS allows for the operator to make certain visual changes to the actual 3D lines and this was used whenever possible to mirror the typologies of lines found in the traditional style of drawing. The experiment started with the most basic of drawing applications—the delineation of the excavation limits—and then progressively moved onward into more specific and detailed applications.

Simultaneously with the above step, each drawing was allotted a unique context number. These numbers were used to directly reference the drawings in the geospatial database—the fourth step of the experiment. The database was based primarily off of that typically found within an archaeological GIS including fields such as: feature material, area (metres squared), and period. Additional fields were needed however to describe certain characteristics that are intrinsic to the single context method of drawing. As such, the fields of perspective, date drawn, drawn by, single context method type, etc. were included within the database. It was also necessary to describe new types of data that were made available by the inclusion of 3D models and drawing in 3D. These fields included associated model and volume (metres cubed) (FIGURE 10). At this point, it can be noted that the fields included are considerably fixed in terms of interpretation. Hodder (1999: 94) suggests that this is a problem with the single context method system of performing archaeology. In order to allow for more fluidity in interpretation, Hodder recommends that some general categories be added to the database (Hodder 1999: 94). This has been accomplished by including an event field where the context may be described either as a 'positive' or 'negative' event. Further interpretation has been encouraged by a field for further description of these events and a field for general comments.

The final step in the experiment was concerned with the visualisation and output of these models. As the models and their 3D features were contained within ArcScene, it was necessary to utilise the 2D and 3D exportation options available in the software.

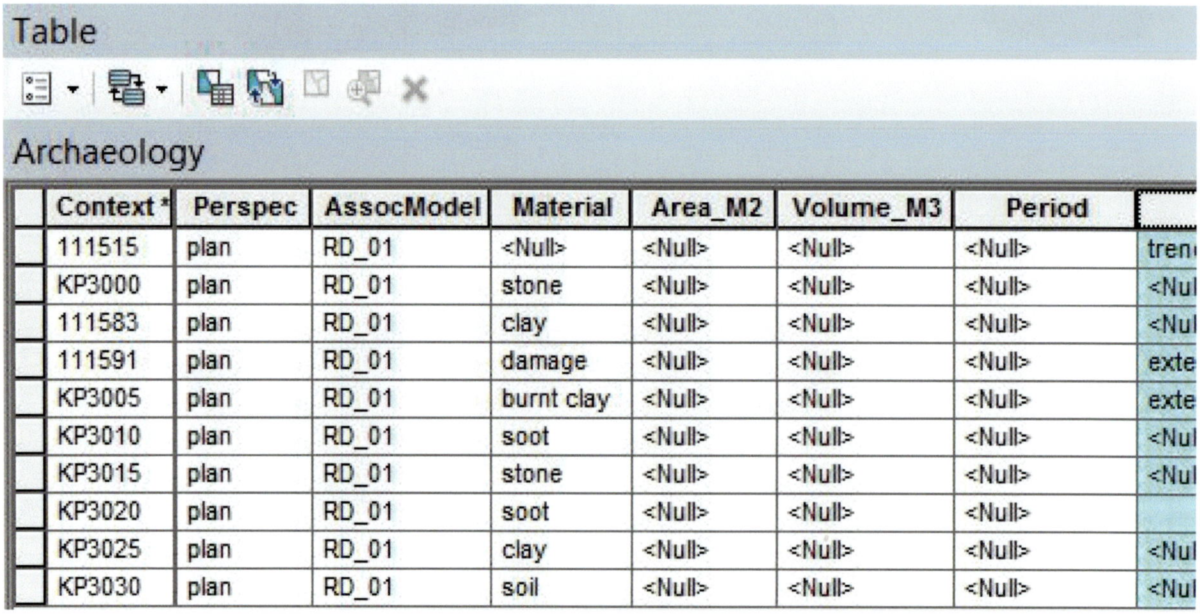

Context	Perspec	AssocModel	Material	Area_M2	Volume_M3	Period	
111515	plan	RD_01	<Null>	<Null>	<Null>	<Null>	tren
KP3000	plan	RD_01	stone	<Null>	<Null>	<Null>	<Nul
111583	plan	RD_01	clay	<Null>	<Null>	<Null>	<Nul
111591	plan	RD_01	damage	<Null>	<Null>	<Null>	exte
KP3005	plan	RD_01	burnt clay	<Null>	<Null>	<Null>	exte
KP3010	plan	RD_01	soot	<Null>	<Null>	<Null>	<Nul
KP3015	plan	RD_01	stone	<Null>	<Null>	<Null>	<Nul
KP3020	plan	RD_01	soot	<Null>	<Null>	<Null>	
KP3025	plan	RD_01	clay	<Null>	<Null>	<Null>	<Nul
KP3030	plan	RD_01	soil	<Null>	<Null>	<Null>	<Nul

FIGURE 10 – A SHORT EXAMPLE OF SOME OF THE DATABASE FIELDS AND VALUES DURING THE INPUT STAGE. (IMAGE BY J.J.L. KIMBALL 2014).

5.6 – Results Concerning 3D Archaeological Drawings

The actual act of 'drawing' in ArcGIS resulted in the production of 3D lines that adhered to the virtual three-dimensional surface of the objects and, thereby, the primary goal of the experiment was successfully realised. As mentioned above, the first attempt at drawing was kept very simple in order to gain an understanding of how the technique works. The simplest object—the excavation limits of Trench 5 that were defined by six points—was attempted first. The tool handled quite predictably for anyone used to drawing with computer programs. After the first initial attempt at drawing on the 3D surface was achieved, the experiment then focused upon testing the competency of drawing in 3D on as many objects as possible. Fortunately, Trench 5 was characterised by a variety of complexities that together yielded a plenteous amount of objects and surfaces, ranging in several 'degrees of drawing difficulty', to serve as a very adequate benchmark test for this technique (FIGURE 11). The extents of smaller simple entities, such as the northern coal/soot layer (context KP3020), were easy to define using the mouse while the extents of the larger contexts were slightly more challenging in that they require the operator to jump back and forth between the drawing and panning tools (FIGURE 12 and FIGURE 13). Some contexts, such as the light-coloured, burnt clay layer (context number 111583, or visually, the horseshoe-shaped feature), represented an even more difficult object to draw upon because of their sharp geometric shapes. This necessitated the operator to zoom in closely and adjust the viewing angle occasionally in order to place the drawing nodes precisely on top of the surface of the model. The most challenging application that this technique was tested with was to draw the packed-stone layer of the oven—a context that is characterised by a series of tightly-spaced stones. All stones were drawn using the 3D drawing tool and although it took a considerable amount of time (about ~50-60 minutes for the approximate ~350 visible stones) to draw compared to other contexts, it was still considerably easy to accomplish (FIGURE 14 and FIGURE 15).

FIGURE 11 – A PHOTOGRAPH DISPLAYING SOME OF THE COMPLEXITIES FACED IN TRENCH 5.
(PHOTOGRAPH © J.J.L. KIMBALL 2013).

FIGURE 12 – (Screen-capture of a 3D Model/3D drawing) This example show the general range of complexities to be drawn; the green polyline denotes a small and relatively non-complex layer whereas the blue polyline denotes a large and complex layer. (Image by J.J.L. Kimball 2014; 3D drawings by J.J.L. Kimball 2014; 3D model by N. Dell'Unto 2013).

FIGURE 13 – (Screen-capture of 3D models/3D drawing) Here the same model and drawings as are displayed in the above figure are shown in their geospatial relation to other 3D models within the GIS. (Image by J.J.L. Kimball 2014; 3D drawings by J.J.L. Kimball 2014; 3D Models and GIS implementation by N. Dell'Unto and the Department of Archaeology and Ancient History, Lund University 2013).

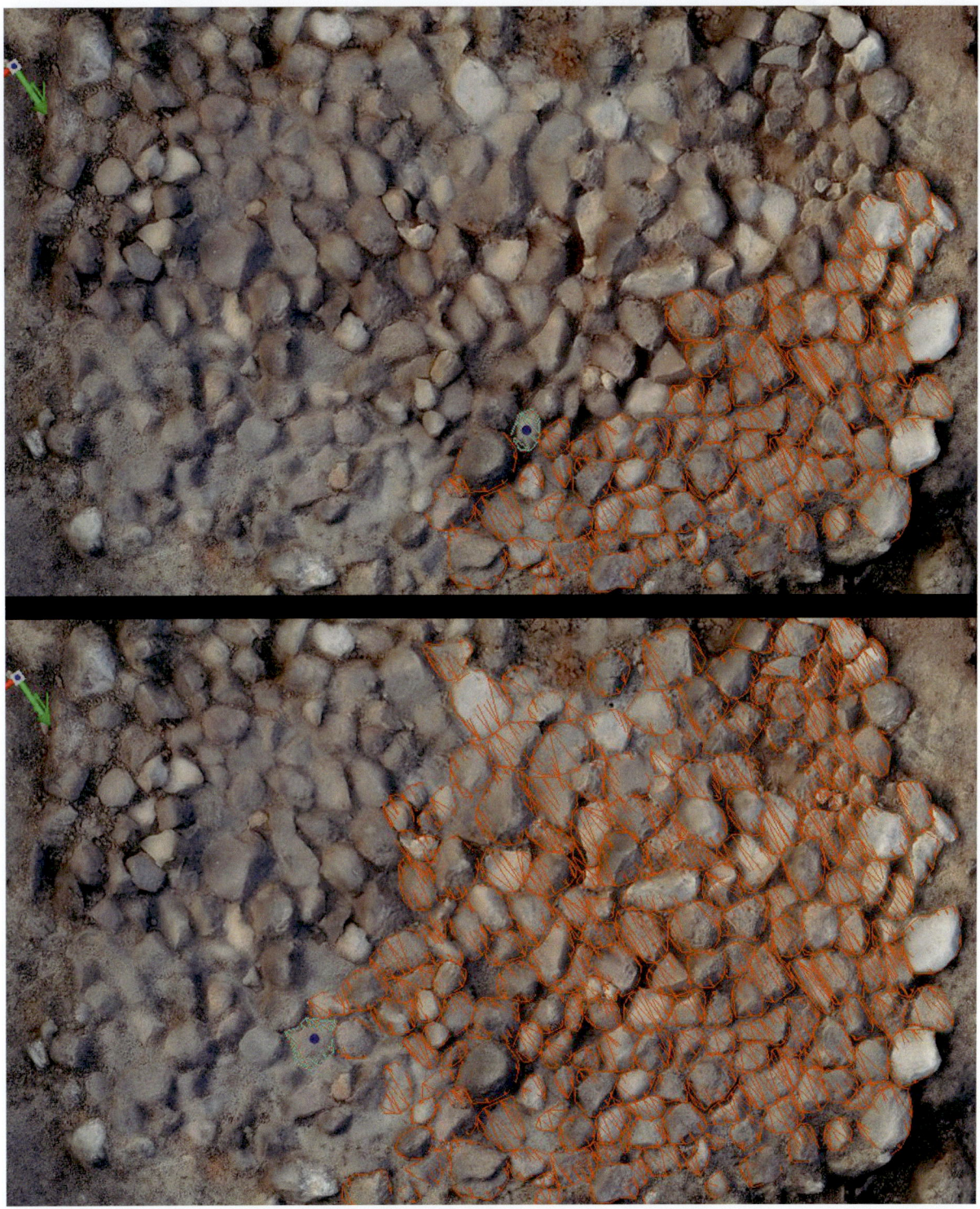

FIGURE 14 – (COMPOSITE SCREEN-CAPTURE IMAGE OF A 3D MODEL/3D DRAWING) AN EXAMPLE SHOWING THE DEVELOPMENT OF THE DRAWING PROCESS OVERTOP OF THE STONE-PACKING LAYER. NOTICE THE INCREASE OF ORANGE POLYLINES BETWEEN THE TOP AND BOTTOM IMAGES. (IMAGE BY J.J.L. KIMBALL 2014; 3D MODEL/3D DRAWINGS BY J.J.L. KIMBALL 2014).

3D Delineation

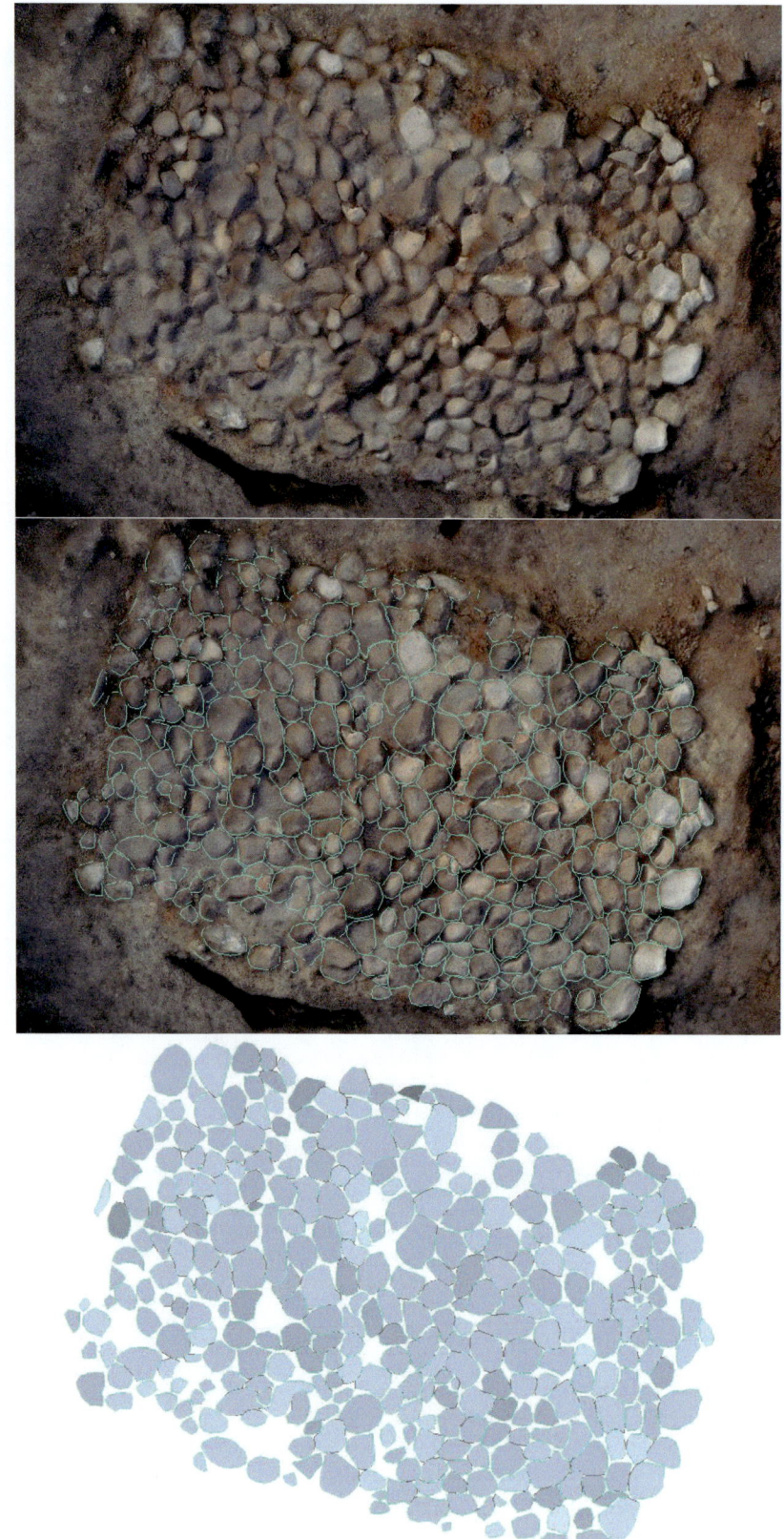

FIGURE 15 – (COMPOSITE SCREEN-CAPTURE IMAGE OF A 3D MODEL SHOWING/3D DRAWING) (I) STONE-PACKING WITH NO DRAWING; (II) STONE-PACKING DELINEATED BY POLYLINES; AND (III) STONE-PACKING VISUALISED ONLY AS POLYGONS. (IMAGES BY J.J.L. KIMBALL 2014; 3D MODELS/3D DRAWINGS BY J.J.L. KIMBALL 2014).

In comparison to the traditional hand-drawn plan, the results of digital drawing look promising. There are notable visual differences between the two drawings, however in theory, the delineation accomplished by 3D drawing should be technically more 'accurate' compared to the plan drawn by hand (FIGURE 16; compare also the location of lines in relation to stones in FIGURE 14 and FIGURE 15).

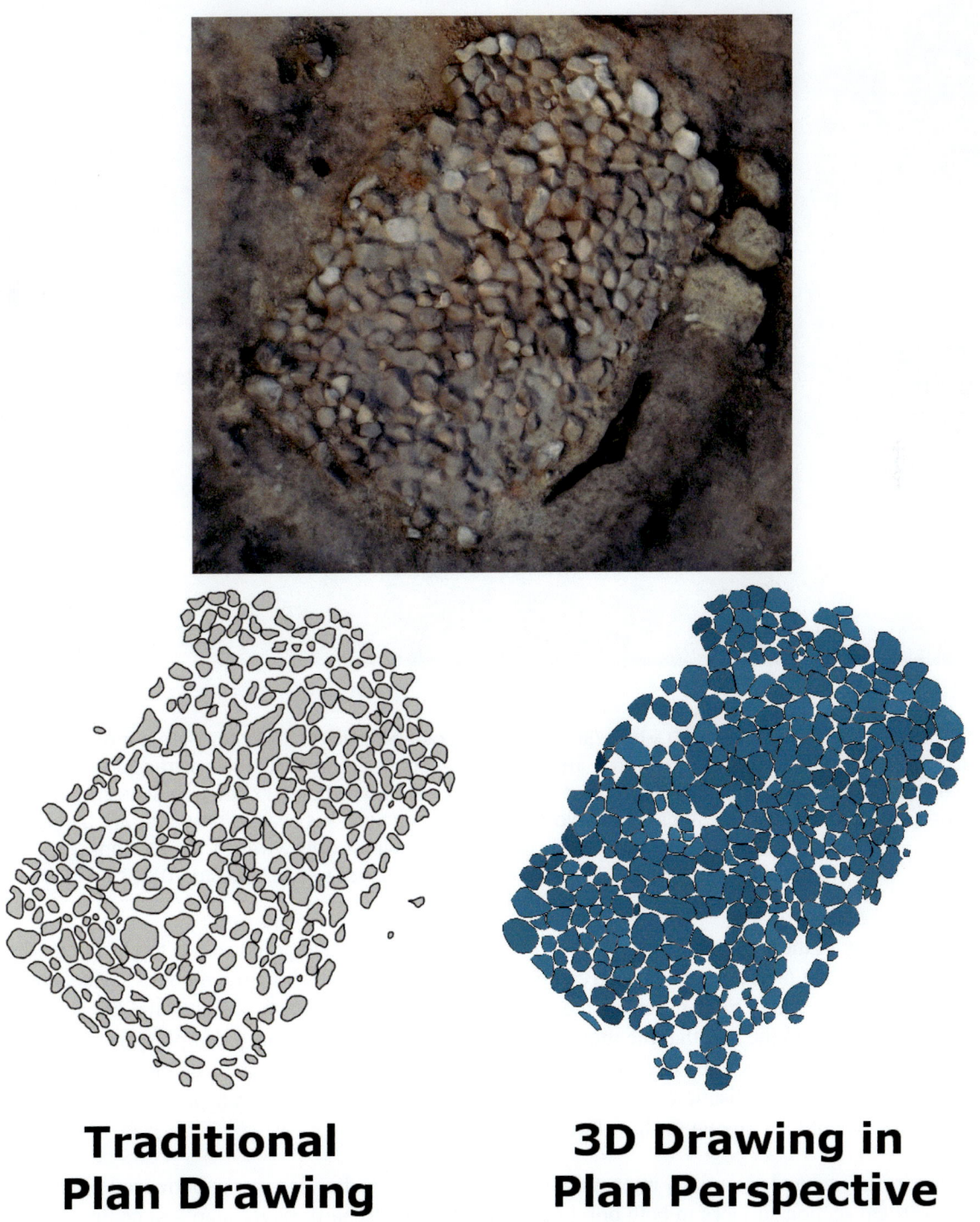

FIGURE 16 – THIS IMAGE SHOWS A COMPARISON BETWEEN TRADITIONAL METHODS AND DIGITAL METHODS. THE TOP IMAGE IS A 3D REPRESENTATION OF THE STONE-PACKING LAYER; TO THE LEFT IS A HAND-DRAWN PLAN; AND TO THE RIGHT IS A 3D DRAWING IN PLAN PERSPECTIVE. (IMAGE BY J.J.L. KIMBALL 2014; 3D MODELS/3D DRAWING BY J.J.L. KIMBALL 2014; HAND-DRAWN PLAN BY J. LUNDIN 2013).

FIGURE 17 – (Screen-capture of 3D model/3D drawing) A composite image showing the relationship between a 3D model and its 3D drawing. Starting in the bottom left corner is an oval shape of the 3D model without any drawings; the next oval shape outward is of the 3D model and its complex polygon geometry in relation to the simple polygons of the 3D drawing—notice that that much of the pink 3D drawings are hidden by the 3D model itself. The outer region shows the 3D drawings only without the 3D model.
(Image by J.J.L. Kimball 2014; 3D models/3D drawings by J.J.L. Kimball 2014).

While drawing in the GIS it became apparent that polygonal drawings produced on top of the model did not necessarily hug the geometry as neatly as expected. Instead of matching the model's surface, portions of polygons may appear hidden behind the texture of the model in some places while being visible in others. This is due to the fact that the model's geometry is significantly more complex than any polygon the operator may feasibly draw overtop the model's surface (FIGURE 17). This can be circumvented by either disabling the visualisation of the 3D model itself or by reducing its transparency to allow for the hidden portions of the drawing to show through the 3D model.

A more frustrating and potentially impacting issue concerning 3D drawing was experienced when drawing upon vertical section surfaces in both polylines and polygons. Regardless if 'snap'—a computer-assisted means of ensuring the mouse cursor, or the click of a mouse, falls precisely upon the closest defined and known point—was enabled or not, it was difficult and even sometimes impossible to get the ArcScene drawing cursor to place the nodes precisely upon vertical surfaces—even if it at first looked like the nodes were placed correctly (FIGURE 18 and FIGURE 19). While this could be remedied by manually

FIGURE 18 – (SCREEN-CAPTURE OF A 3D MODEL/3D DRAWING; SECTION PERSPECTIVE) THIS IMAGE WAS CAPTURED DURING THE DRAWING PROCESS. AT FIRST GLANCE, ONE MIGHT BELIEVE THAT THESE NODES HAVE BEEN ACCURATELY PLACED UPON THE SURFACE OF THE MODEL, ALLOWING FOR THE SUCCESSFUL DEVELOPMENT OF A POLYGON.
(IMAGE BY J.J.L. KIMBALL 2014; 3D MODEL/3D DRAWINGS BY J.J.L. KIMBALL 2014).

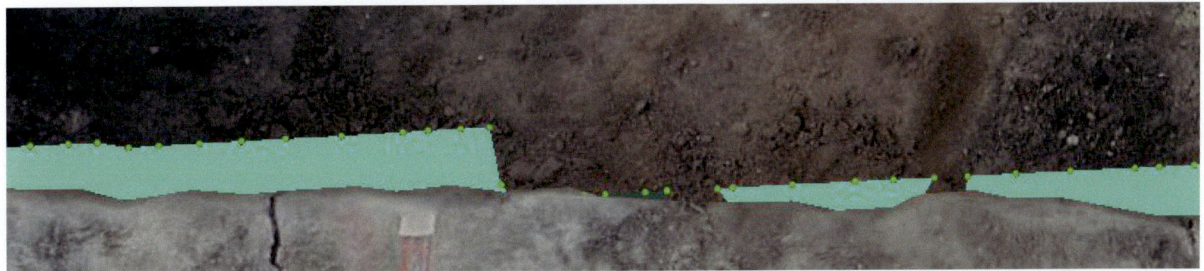

FIGURE 19 – (SCREEN-CAPTURE OF A 3D MODEL/3D DRAWING; SLIGHTLY OBLIQUE PLAN PERSPECTIVE) THIS IMAGE WAS CAPTURED AFTER THE DRAWING PROCESS HAD BEEN COMPLETED. ON CLOSER INSPECTION, SOME NODES HAVE 'LIFTED' OFF OF THE SURFACE, CREATING A VERY TEDIOUS TASK TO RELOCATE THEM INTO THEIR INTENDED POSITIONS. TWO BREAKS IN THE POLYGON CAN ALSO BE SEEN CENTRE TO CENTRE RIGHT (IMAGE BY J.J.L. KIMBALL 2014; 3D MODEL/3D DRAWINGS BY J.J.L. KIMBALL 2014).

adjusting the x or y value of the nodes in order to ensure they were placed precisely, this workaround was considerably labour intensive—particularly because each point must be adjusted individually in order to align it with the corresponding location upon the model's surface. Furthermore, while polyline shapefiles resulted in a 3D drawing that was clearly what one would consider to be a 'line', polygon shapefiles were prone to producing geometries that did not always conform to the sequentially ordered placement of their nodes (FIGURE 20, see also FIGURE 18 and FIGURE 19). Despite many hours of attempting to troubleshoot the problem, no feasible solution was found. Thus most sections (with the exception of a small set of sections, cf. FIGURE 21) were instead drawn in polylines—an unfortunate compromise as most individual layers in archaeological section drawings are denoted by some form of unique fill which is not an intrinsic property of the polyline.

The single-context method for drawing was followed as closely as possible, however there were difficulties stemming from the nature of the software itself. Since ArcGIS is not oriented specifically towards archaeological applications, the drawing tool does not have all of the line symbols used in the

FIGURE 20 – (SCREEN-CAPTURE OF A 3D DRAWING; SECTION PERSPECTIVE) THIS IMAGE WAS CAPTURED AFTER THE DRAWING PROCESS HAD BEEN COMPLETED. A MAJOR DRAWBACK OF DRAWING IN 3D WITH POLYGONS IS THAT THE POLYGON IS PROJECTED AS INDIVIDUALLY SEGREGATED PIECES—NOTE THE SHADING DIFFERENCES AND MOST SIGNIFICANTLY THE SEVEN WHITE SPACES BETWEEN. (IMAGE BY J.J.L. KIMBALL 2014; 3D DRAWING BY J.J.L. KIMBALL 2014).

FIGURE 21 – (SCREEN-CAPTURE OF A 3D MODEL/3D DRAWING) THE ONLY EXAMPLES WHERE POLYGONS WERE USED SUCCESSFULLY TO DISTINGUISH BETWEEN LAYERS. THE MODEL ITSELF HAS BEEN MADE MORE TRANSPARENT TO HELP THE READER SEE THE COMPLETE EXTENTS OF THE SECTION DRAWINGS (IMAGE BY J.J.L. KIMBALL 2014; 3D DRAWINGS BY J.J.L. KIMBALL 2014; 3D MODEL BY N. DELL'UNTO).

single-context method. A potential work-around to this problem would be the development of unique line types via the symbol property editor. It is unfortunate, however, that many of these line types in the property editor appear to only function reliably in two-dimensional applications—a factor that effectively renders these useless for drawing in three-dimensions. The solution that was utilised was to use those lines available in ArcGIS's drawing tool that worked in 3D and that corresponded most with those line types as set by the single-context method. Despite these difficulties, the action of drawing was performed on all objects that would have traditionally been drawn in plan (e.g. excavation limits, and extent of contexts and features) and drawn in section (e.g. the stratigraphy in profile) in a fashion that is not unlike the current documentation methods employed at Uppåkra in the present day (compare FIGURE 22 with FIGURE 23).

Finally, because the inclusion of 3D models into a GIS resulted in a 3D/4D GIS, the drawings also inherently became part of this system. This enables one to transcend the traditional means of viewing archaeological documentation, and to view more closely to how it actually existed on the site—as a 3D entity tied directly to other 3D entities around it. Furthermore, since these models can be stacked upon one another chronologically, so too are the drawings that are associated with those individual models. Thus one can toggle on and off the visibility of the drawing layers in order to see how the archaeology of those layers progressed in quick succession. In other words, one can select a model of a chronologically earlier phase of the excavation and adjust its transparency to show a chronologically later phase underneath (FIGURE 24 and FIGURE 25). The final results for drawing all archaeological features in Trench 5 are displayed in FIGURE 26, FIGURE 27, and FIGURE 28. While the results of drawing in 3D can most easily be visualised directly through GIS itself, if needed, these drawings can be exported into either a two-dimensional format (e.g. JPG, TIFF, or PDF) or a three-dimensional format (VRML). Unfortunately, the 3D exportation option is limited to a type of file that only deals with vector graphics—and so the ability to effortlessly share the raster data viewable within the GIS is limited. For the time being, there does not appear to be a method to export multipatch files from ArcScene into a common file format like PDF.

In conclusion, the experiment showed that there are indeed applications for 3D models beyond the production of a 3D/4D GIS. When input into the excavation GIS, it is possible to more fully integrate these models by using their geometries to create new 3D data. The 3D data produced through this action can then be assigned attributes and linked into the geodatabase which again deepens the connection between 3D models and other archaeological data.[4]

---

[4] Many of the aspects discussed above are best demonstrated through a short video which can be found under the title of "3D Archaeological Drawings" in the linked webpage: https://sites.google.com/site/justinjlkimball/masters-data

3D Delineation

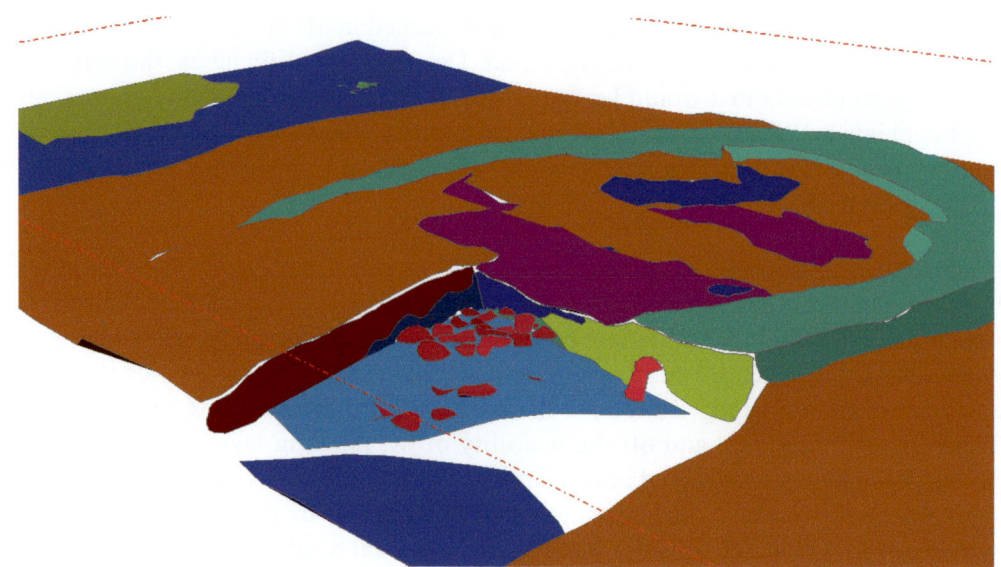

FIGURE 22 – (SCREEN-CAPTURE OF 3D DRAWINGS). THIS IMAGE SHOWS A VARIETY OF CONTEXTS AND SECTIONS PROJECTED IN THE SAME ENVIRONMENT AND IN RELATION TO ONE ANOTHER. (IMAGE AND 3D DRAWING BY J.J.L. KIMBALL 2014. REFERENCE 3D MODEL BY N. DELL'UNTO 2013).

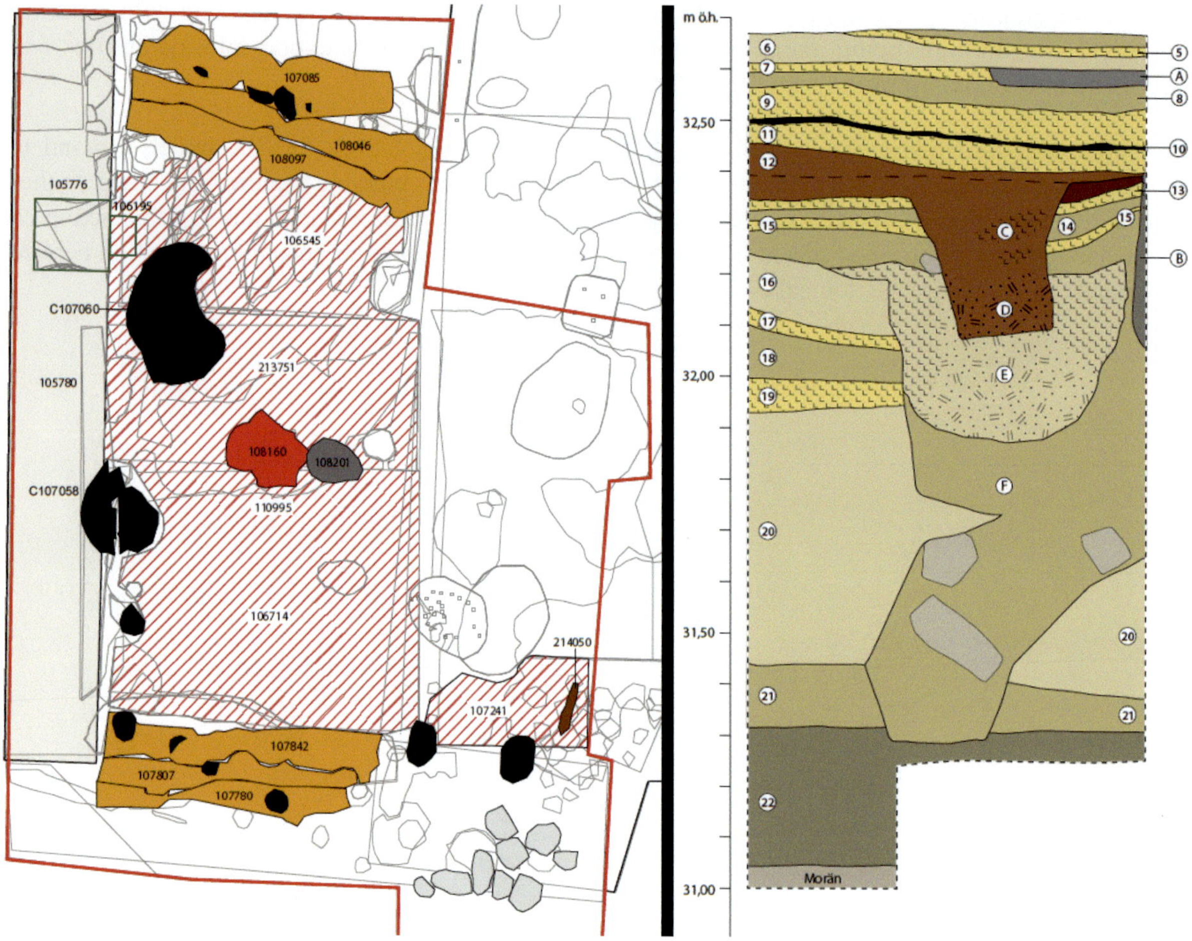

FIGURE 23 – (SCREEN-CAPTURE) HERE ARE TWO EXAMPLES OF THE CURRENT DRAWING METHODOLOGY AT UPPÅKRA. [LEFT] A PLAN DRAWING OF CONTEXTS ACQUIRED VIA TOTAL STATION; [RIGHT] A DIGITISED SECTION DRAWING. BY DESIGN THESE DRAWINGS MUST BE VIEWED OUT OF CONTEXT FROM ONE ANOTHER (IMAGES BY SÖDERBERG ET AL. 2014).

Experiment: 3D Delineation

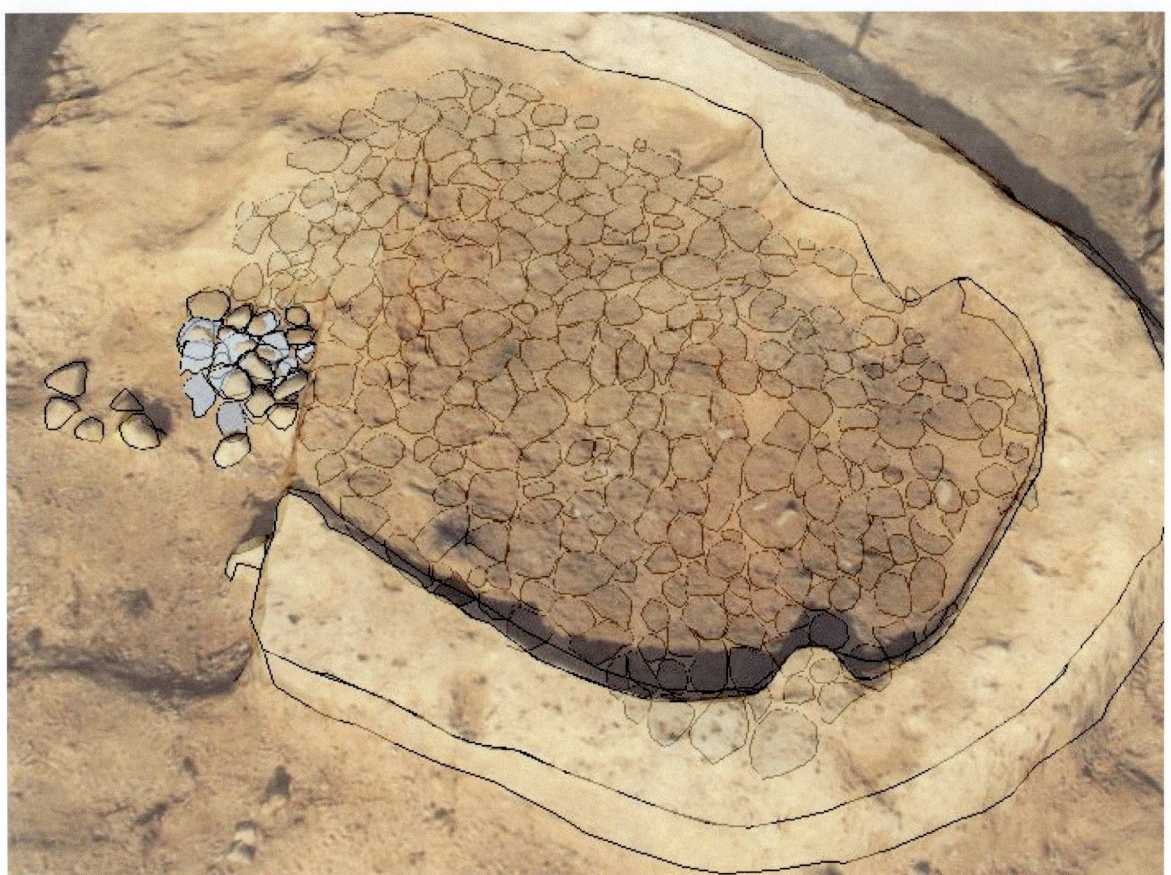

FIGURE 24 – (SCREEN-CAPTURE OF A 3D MODEL/3D DRAWING) AN EXAMPLE OF CHRONOLOGICAL LAYERING: A MODEL OF A YOUNGER PHASE OF THE EXCAVATION IS REDUCED IN TRANSPARENCY AND SUPERIMPOSED OVER TOP OF A DRAWING OF ROCK-PACKING (AN OLDER PHASE). (IMAGE AND 3D DRAWING BY J.J.L. KIMBALL 2014; 3D MODEL BY N. DELL'UNTO).

FIGURE 25 – (SCREEN-CAPTURE OF 3D MODELS) ANOTHER EXAMPLE OF CHRONOLOGICAL LAYERING: THIS TIME THE OVERLAYING 3D MODEL IS SIGNIFICANTLY REDUCED IN TRANSPARENCY SO THAT THE BASE MODEL CAN BE SEEN. TO HELP DELINEATE THE LOCATION OF THE OVERLAY MODEL'S FEATURES, A DRAWN OUTLINE HAS BEEN PROVIDED. (IMAGE BY J.J.L. KIMBALL 2014; BASE 3D MODEL BY J.J.L. KIMBALL 2014; OVERLAY 3D MODEL BY N. DELL'UNTO).

FIGURE 26 – (SCREEN-CAPTURE OF 3D MODEL/3D DRAWING) HERE THE 3D DRAWING HAS BEEN SLIGHTLY TRANSPARENT AND OVERLAYED ON TOP OF THE FIRST 3D MODEL OF TRENCH 5. (IMAGE AND 3D DRAWING BY J.J.L. KIMBALL 2014; 3D MODEL BY N. DELL'UNTO).

Experiment: 3D Delineation

Figure 27 – (Screen-capture of 3D model/3D drawing) The top image shows completed 3D drawing for the second 3D model of Trench 5. The bottom image shows a transparent overlay of the 3D drawing overtop of 3D model. (Images by J.J.L. Kimball 2014; 3D models/3D drawings by J.J.L. Kimball 2014).

3D Delineation

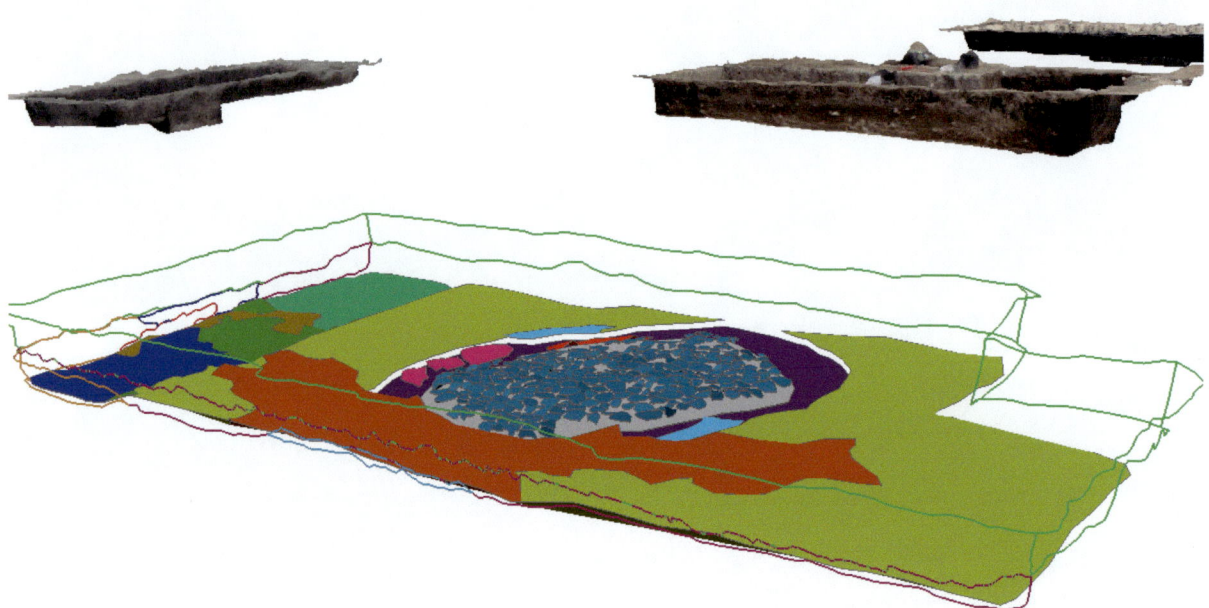

FIGURE 28 – (Screen-capture of 3D models) 3D drawings of the latest stage of excavations in Trench 5 displayed in their geospatial relation to other 3D models within the GIS. (Image and 3D drawing by J.J.L. Kimball 2014; Base 3D model for Trench 5 by J.J.L. Kimball 2014, all other 3D Models and GIS implementation by N. Dell'Unto and the Department of Archaeology and Ancient History, Lund University 2013).

6 – Discussion

The goal of this work has been to define one potential application that explores beyond the simple production of a 3D/4D GIS using models created through MSR, in order to experiment with the intrinsic capabilities of GIS to make those models more relevant for archaeological applications. This was accomplished by developing a synthesis between a new technology and an old technology. The unison between these two technologies resulted in a method that combines the interpretative power of archaeological drawing and the realistic visualisation capabilities of 3D digital models into a single powerful package. This package not only helps to communicate what the archaeologist deems as important, but also results in the creation of new forms of data which can be woven along with other information within the geodatabase. As a recap, the process was broken down into five steps: 1) the creation of the 3D digital models through MSR; 2) the introduction of those 3D digital models into the excavation GIS to establish a 3D/4D GIS; 3) the actual drawing in 3D overtop of those models within the GIS itself; 4) the linking of those drawings into the GIS database; and finally followed by 5) the visualisation and output of those models and drawings in various 2D and 3D formats. These steps together represent a methodology for an archaeologically-relevant application of 3D digital models in a manner that enables archaeologists to comprehend, interpret, visualise, and disseminate archaeological information within a timeframe congruent with the constraints endemic to field archaeology.

More specifically, there are many significant findings that have been made apparent through this methodology. One such finding is in reference to the actual act of drawing, in that drawing in 3D upon a 3D digital model forces the archaeologist to think in the terms of the natural three-dimensional world. In other words, this technique is a direct response to the call for 3D solutions for 3D problems. Unlike the traditional method of plan drawing, where one uses a plumb bob and measuring stick to determine the two-dimensional location of features within a grid, three-dimensional drawing requires the user to think and perform the act of drawing in 3D. To ensure that one achieves the desired results of drawing, their perspective of the object must be occasionally manipulated—they must move, bob, and weave throughout the act of drawing. As a consequence, the individual must actively traverse the object and develop some sense of its geometry while ensuring that their line falls where they want it to. In this regard, the nature of the model forces the archaeologist to re-experience it. Furthermore, the 3D digital model itself affords the archaeologist with unique vantage points that may otherwise be difficult, impossible, or even risky/dangerous (to either the archaeologist or the archaeology itself). This technique may therefore allow some features to be documented in detail that may have otherwise not been documented at all.

Another consideration is that this technique can be applied in the performance of both archaeological and plan section drawings. While there is a limited capability to reproduce certain typologies of lines that are defined by the single-context method (cf. Museum of London Archaeological Service 1994 and FIGURE 1 at the beginning of this work) in the drawing tool of ArcGIS, I believe that the actual nature of documenting and drawing in 3D upon a 3D representation is beginning to abrogate the need for such symbolically-laden line typologies—after all, those very symbolically-laden lines were targeted toward conveying 3D characteristics upon a 2D medium (again, e.g. paper). Instead of relying upon such symbolic line types, an archaeologist equipped with a 3D model adorned with archaeologically-relevant 3D drawings only has to change her/his own perspective in order to understand and appreciate visually the 3D characteristics of the object. Of course, it is still important for the interpretation that such information be included apart from the model itself. This can be directly accomplished by adding a section to the attributes table where the archaeologist may include keywords describing—via text—the type of and/or relationship between contexts present in the features. Furthermore, this enables the archaeologist to query for archaeological objects with certain context relationships as defined by their keywords (e.g. cut by context #, seals context #, etc.).

In addition to the above consideration, another finding of interest relates to the two 2D typologies of archaeological drawing: plans and sections. Since 3D digital models occupy a three-dimensional space, both types of archaeological drawings can be visualised immediately within the same space and in relation to each other. Before, such visualisations could only be linked together via text or certain line types (e.g. in the single-context planning method, a section would be recorded on the plan with a dashed line denoted by the section identity number above the line). With this methodology, it is again as simple as changing the perspective in order to achieve a fully-visualised superimposition of the drawing *in situ* overtop of the feature.

The act of drawing directly into a computer also has its own benefits. Most evident perhaps is that computer software offers the opportunity for a 'cleaner' end result (e.g. no eraser marks, dirt, mud, or (accidental) coffee stains, etc.). Furthermore, because the medium is digital in nature, there is no need to digitise the drawing via a document scanner. Another benefit is that 3D drawings done within ArcScene are recorded as vector graphics, thereby permitting the archaeologist to zoom in or out without sacrificing the quality of the drawing due to pixilation (mathematical algorithms intrinsic within vector graphics technically allow for infinite zoom without loss in detail, compared to raster data which is limited to a specific resolution made up of a large, albeit finite, number of pixels as data). Scanned versions of archaeological drawings do not initially allow for this because scanners are raster-based devices—if the benefit of vector-based graphics was desired, the archaeologist would be required to *redraw* the archaeological drawing; thereby adding *even more* time to an already time-consuming process. Another benefit relating to digital drawings, especially in a geometrically referenced space, relates to the ability to perform measurements. In ArcScene, a handy feature called 'Measure' allows for one to perform a variety of measurements on both their 3D models and their 3D drawings. For example, the measure tool allows for one to measure a direct line between two points, the height of objects, the area of an object, and the distance around a feature (FIGURE 29). While this tool could be useful at any given moment, its particular worth can be appreciated when one recognises that it can allow for the measurement of 3D modelled features long after they have been destroyed by the process of archaeology.

Not so surprisingly, yet still profound nonetheless, was that drawing in 3D was found to expedite the act of archaeological drawing. Another benefit was that the drawings seemed to have a high congruency between what was actually visible on the model itself and what was drawn in the software. Thus, drawing in 3D on a digital medium is both efficient and accurate. Others have already explored the benefits of drawing in digital mediums (cf. Cianciarulo and Guerra 2007; Prins and Adams 2012), however, these researchers have restricted their drawings to two-dimensions only. The methodology demonstrated in the experiment must not be confused with these attempts as it has accomplished digital drawings in three-dimensions. Regardless, there are definitely similarities between 2D and 3D digital drawings—such as not having to position one's self awkwardly around the object (and thereby avoid risking damage to the feature and one's self) or fumble with cumbersome or unwieldy measuring instruments to produce the archaeological drawing. This of course increases the accuracy and quality, while reducing the time it takes to develop the drawings. Unique to drawing in 3D, however, is that the archaeologist can move the virtual perspective as needed—the mobility of which affords a complete 3D perspective of the archaeological object being recorded. Even those who are less-artistically competent should feel comfortable with this technique as it involves simply tracing out what is visible. Yet it is still important to stress the speed in which it takes to complete these drawings. The traditional methodology concerned with producing archaeological drawings is known to take a considerable amount of time when done correctly, thereby it is usually reserved for those features and contexts perceived as having significant value. With the same amount of care, but minus the time one needs to take to fiddle with bulky measuring instruments, one can achieve similar results housed *within* a 3D environment—all within the timeframe of the excavation.

DISCUSSION

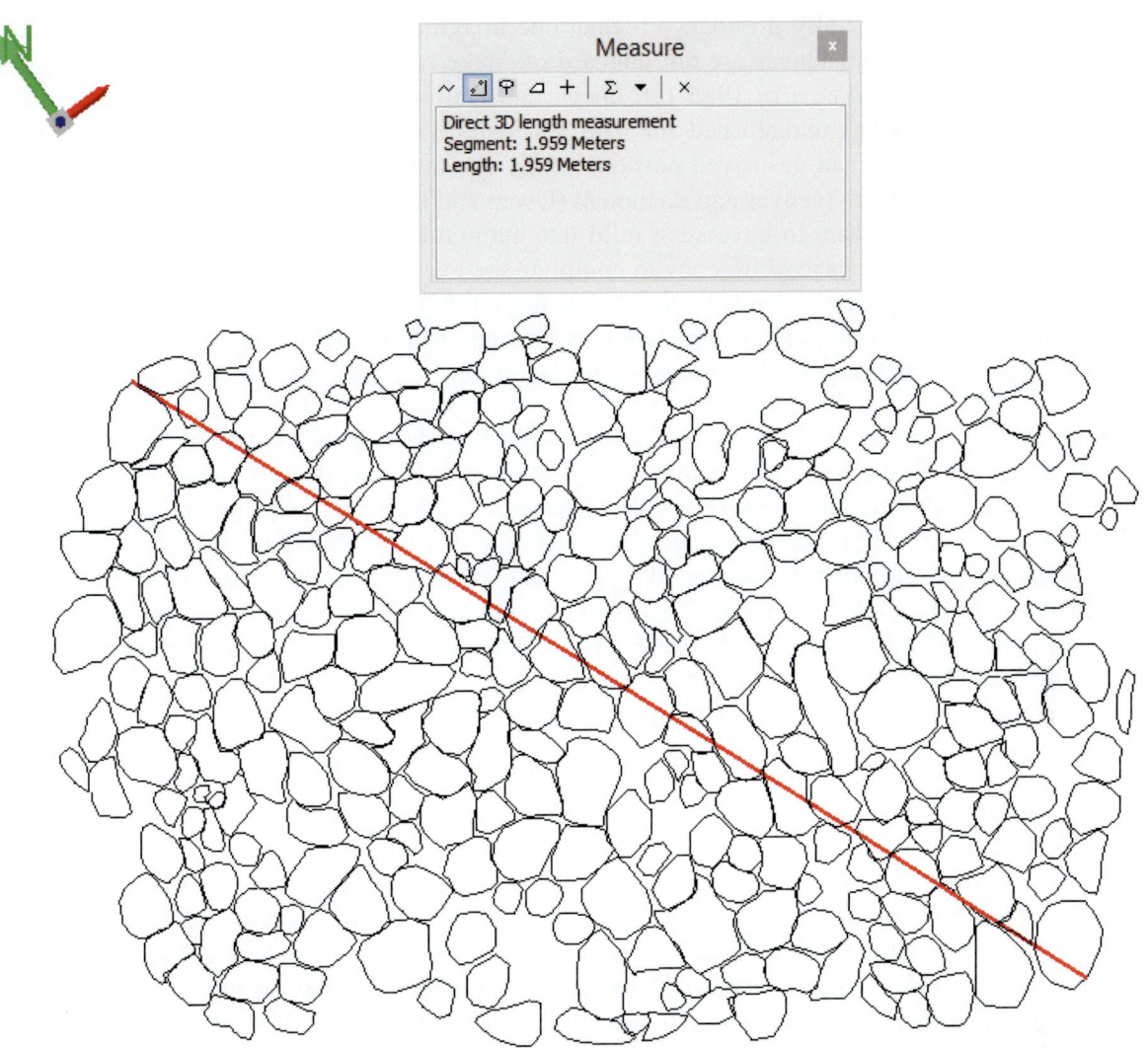

FIGURE 29 – (SCREEN-CAPTURE OF A 3D DRAWING) ONE OF THE MEASURE TOOL FEATURES IN ARCSCENE: HERE THE TOOL HAS BEEN USED TO MEASURE DIAGONALLY ACROSS THE STONE-PACKING LAYER WHICH PROVIDES A RESULT OF 1.959 METERS ACROSS. (IMAGE BY J.J.L. KIMBALL 2014; REFERENCE 3D MODEL/3D DRAWING BY J.J.L. KIMBALL 2014).

A supplementary note to the above paragraph is that some concerns may arise, reflecting those cautioned by Barker on photography, in that drawing in a digital space may remove the archaeologist away from the actual archaeology before them. This issue is indeed valid; however, it is somewhat more valid for 2D digital drawing than it is for 3D digital drawing. Drawing in 2D restricts the archaeologist by constricting their perspective to one plane. 3D on the other hand allows for the archaeologist to explore the scene—to change their perspective whether that be the angle of view and/or the amount of magnification. Regardless, it is important for the archaeologist to perform these tasks in front of the object being documented if at all possible. This allows for the archaeologist to check the model to ensure it is an acceptable representation of the archaeology while at the same time offering a valuable source of reference to compare their drawing against.

For archaeologists concerned with rescue and development-led archaeology, the truncation in time it takes to document cannot be overemphasised. When time and money are a serious issue, this methodology can be applied in order to conduct the art of archaeological drawing outside of the excavation itself. The value of the ability to accomplish such a task after the excavation phase or even after the entire excavation itself has passed, becomes especially pronounced when one imagines a situation where the archaeology itself is threatened. Such instances are not unheard of—take for example the discovery of the Scar boat burial, located in Orkney, in 1985 (cf. Owen and Dalland 1999). The site, discovered by a non-archaeologist, was left undisturbed for over six years until its significance was realised. By this time, coastal erosion had destroyed portions of the site and what was left was threatened by a shrinking amount of time to recover and document (Owen and Dalland 1999: 1-2; Towrie 2014). The archaeologists were fortunate to have such mild late autumn/early winter weather on the site, and although there was a real sense of urgency to complete the excavation before the conditions soured, they were able to complete drawings of the archaeology (Owen and Dalland 1999: 25 and 30). In circumstances such as this, where the archaeological documentation process itself is either rushed or unable to be conducted properly, the application of the established methodology holds much promise.

Another example of the above situation has been noted at Çatalhöyük. The nature of the construction material that make up the buildings uncovered at Çatalhöyük is considerably unstable. This makes conservation difficult and thus one response has been to make an effort to document these buildings (Forte et al. 2012: 374-376). Yet another useful application that is of chief benefit to those concerned with rescue and development-led archaeology, is that 3D digital models and 3D archaeological drawing allows for a detailed and powerful way of documenting layers of an excavation that, because of time or financial limitations, must be destroyed in order to reach layers deemed more significant. Thus in both of these examples, the documentation of the threatened archaeology in 3D may be the only chance that archaeologists have to perform the important task of creating archaeological drawings.

A final consideration is in reference towards *who* should be exercising the technique of 3D archaeological drawing. My response to this falls in line with Hodder's reflexive methodology of excavation practice: it should be the *individual excavators* that use this technique. After all, they are the ones that actively experience the site through the act of excavation. Therefore, 3D archaeological drawings are a tool that must be applied, first and foremost, by those very same individuals because they have the knowledge to describe most accurately all of the features they encounter (and especially those contexts that are virtually invisible to the eye, yet tactually evident). Indeed, 3D archaeological drawing is a tool that *must* be completed whenever possible in the field and by those individuals performing the action of excavating. In addition to these factors, giving the excavators control over this technology functions to further bring the voice of the humble field archaeologist from behind the scenes and into a more forefront position. As noted by Hodder (1999: 94), putting techniques such as this in the hands of the field archaeologist increases mutlivocality and thereby adds to the fullness of the resulting interpretation. Ensuring that the excavating archaeologist has command over this technique presents another important factor: it places this technique in the frontlines of archaeology where interpretation happens as trowel meets earth (Hodder 1999: 94).

The ability to conduct archaeological drawings in 3D is a technique that must not be understated. With many benefits, (e.g. enabling the archaeologist to approach the three-dimensional nature of the site with a three-dimensional documentation method; allowing for the visualisation of previously disjointed objects (e.g. plan and section drawings, also photographs) in relation to one another in the same space; providing expedited and more accurate drawings; and increasing multivocality by giving the individual excavator a greater voice), it is irrefutable that 3D digital models are a useful typology of data that must be considered more closely as being relevant for archaeological knowledge. This statement is unequivocal when supported by the experiment above; one that has demonstrated that drawing upon 3D models allows for a more powerful and communicative form of archaeological documentation that is itself within a three-dimensional medium and therefore better representative of 'reality' compared to other formats of documentation.

6.1 – Statement of Perceived Impact

> "It is wisdom to recognize necessity, when all other courses have been weighed . . ."
> Spoken by Gandalf the Grey in *The Fellowship of the Ring*
> (J. R. R. Tolkien 2008: 201).

Throughout this work, especially within the state of art section, I have maintained a stance where digital technologies must not be seen as supplanting traditional technologies. Adherence to this statement is vital for archaeology because the history of our practice defines what we endeavour to achieve today. However, another underlying theme has been present the entire time—that which acknowledges technological *evolution*. Archaeology has not been a stranger to these processes: cameras have moved from film to memory cards; technology has long existed to create digital copies of paper documentation; paper databases have become digitised allowing for a variety of new processes—the list goes on. Yet despite the digitisation of such technologies, they have fundamentally remained the same: digital cameras still involve the capture of photons upon a light-sensitive surface in order to produce representations of the scene before them; digital documents still need to be authored or created through great forethought and a synthesis of data and ideas; and databases, such as GISs, still depend on the input of vast amounts of data. While the technologies have changed, and to some extent their methodologies have changed, their involvement in our endeavours are more present than ever. They have not been supplanted—rather if anything, we have come to depend upon them more than ever. The continual digitisation of our technology is, at least in the near future, unstoppable. Thus it is the wisest course of action to continually keep an open, but cautious, mind towards understanding how newer technologies work. In other words, we must allow ourselves to embrace new technology while also remaining grounded enough to take the time to explore the methodologies and applications for those new technologies within the whole of archaeological theory and practice. Through such actions, a more reflexive and enriching archaeology can be achieved than would be possible if one were to remain purely in either extreme regarding technology.

That having been stated, it is therefore relevant and necessary that archaeologists must begin looking for ways to update and modernise the discipline of archaeology—in order to bring the discipline into the 21st century. One manner in which this can be jumpstarted is for archaeologists to begin to more earnestly embrace 3D documentation technologies. Paper, pencils, and erasers have already begun to disappear from our modern world in favour of smart phones, tablets, and laptops. I do not however suggest nor recommend archaeologists to cast traditional technologies completely aside. After all, there certainly is relevance in teaching children how to write with a pencil, just as there will certainly be a relevance and richness provided through the continual instruction of students in the 'basic' two-dimensional techniques of archaeology (Campana 2014: 7). Undoubtedly there will be a time in every archaeologist's career where such 'mundane' technologies become the saviours for documentation in field excavation—particular stories such as mobile phones being inhumed in trenches, digital cameras falling into buckets of water, or a total station's (unintentional yet surely dramatic) attempt at flight from the top of a cliff come specifically to mind (Backhouse 2006: 45). While instances such as these are persuasive on their own for retaining knowledge of manual documentation techniques, it is also equally relevant for archaeologists to be aware of the continually developing history of archaeological practice—because, and I purposely repeat myself for emphasis, the performance of archaeology is solely dependent on the trials, tribulations, successes, failures, and achievements of the past. It was the desire to capture more accurately the past that caused the trowel to become utilised in certain applications over the shovel. It was then this detail, provided through the use of a tool commanding more finesse than others, that necessitated specific ways to document what was seen and experienced—and so on and so forth. In addition, technological advancements may also directly *enable* more readily the act of documentation.

3D Delineation

The late Philip Barker, while discussing vertical stereoscopic photography in his book *Techniques of Archaeological Excavation*, recognised this very fact, well in advance of his time, when he stated that:

> "What is needed is an accurate record of the excavated surfaces, features and structures. If photography can provide this record, *in colour and in three-dimensions*, it is arguable that detailed site drawing, in the accepted sense, is superfluous, and that the drawing can be confined to outline overlays, which include all the context numbers. Such a system would enormously speed up the recording of all kinds of site . . . where it has become customary to draw the surface in great detail and then to colour each element" [italic emphasis mine]
>
> P. Barker (1993: 185).

Barker clearly recognised the potential that technological advancements had for the production of archaeological documentation. Anyone who has read Barker's book knows that he is consistently clear that archaeological documentation must be done with meticulous care in order to ensure it is of usable quality in the future. Based on the above quotation, Barker would have likely recommended such techniques and methodologies that enabled the precise and inclusive documentation of data such as those involving 3D technologies—after all, 3D digital models and the act of outlining overlays and attaching context numbers to those is exactly what has been accomplished in this work's experiment. What must be understood is that digital documentation techniques, such as the one defined above, cannot supplant traditional technologies because they represent modern manners of performing the same techniques. Therefore, it is important that we embrace such technological advances—so long as we continue to pay homage towards their origins and make an effort to understand the technological origins of the modern digital technologies that we apply.

6.1.1 – Guidelines and Symbologies for 3D Archaeological Drawing

With that having been stated, what is necessary then is to establish a set of guidelines for 3D archaeological drawing. The issue with drawing in three-dimensions is that many mediums currently utilised today are limited to two dimensions (take for example this work which has consistently been attempting to demonstrate 3D objects with 2D imagery). Thus there must be some kind of format available to archaeologists that wish to draw in 3D but also need to distribute those drawings in a 2D medium. My intention was to provide a solution that closely followed the symbology of the single context method of archaeological drawing (Museum of London Archaeological Service 1994), but constructed as line types directly inside of ArcScene itself. ESRI's ArcGIS does allow for complex lines to be formed that involve multiple line elements made from a variety of angles. Whereas I was able to reconstruct all line types in ESRI's ArcGIS, these lines only functioned in the 2D ArcMap platform rather than in the 3D ArcScene platform. The problem seems to stem from an inability of ArcScene to project line types that are of a complex nature—in other words, anything beyond simple, singular cartographic solid or dash format lines (FIGURE 30). There is an inherent difficulty with translating languages: an idiom from one language directly translated into another language and then again directly translated back into the first, never captures the essence of the original idiom. It would seem then, that this is one of those circumstances where a 2D language used to describe 3D features cannot itself be cohesively translated into a 3D language itself.

Although somewhat frustrating, these limitations can be somewhat circumvented. For example, planned documentation at Uppåkra has already been achieved over many years with a limited palette of line types. Furthermore, the attribute tables, as described above, also allow the user to input data that describes what a cut or edge looks like. Finally, the archaeologist can produce a variety of screenshots from multiple angles to bring to the reader's attention what those edges and cuts looked like in 3D. Keeping these features

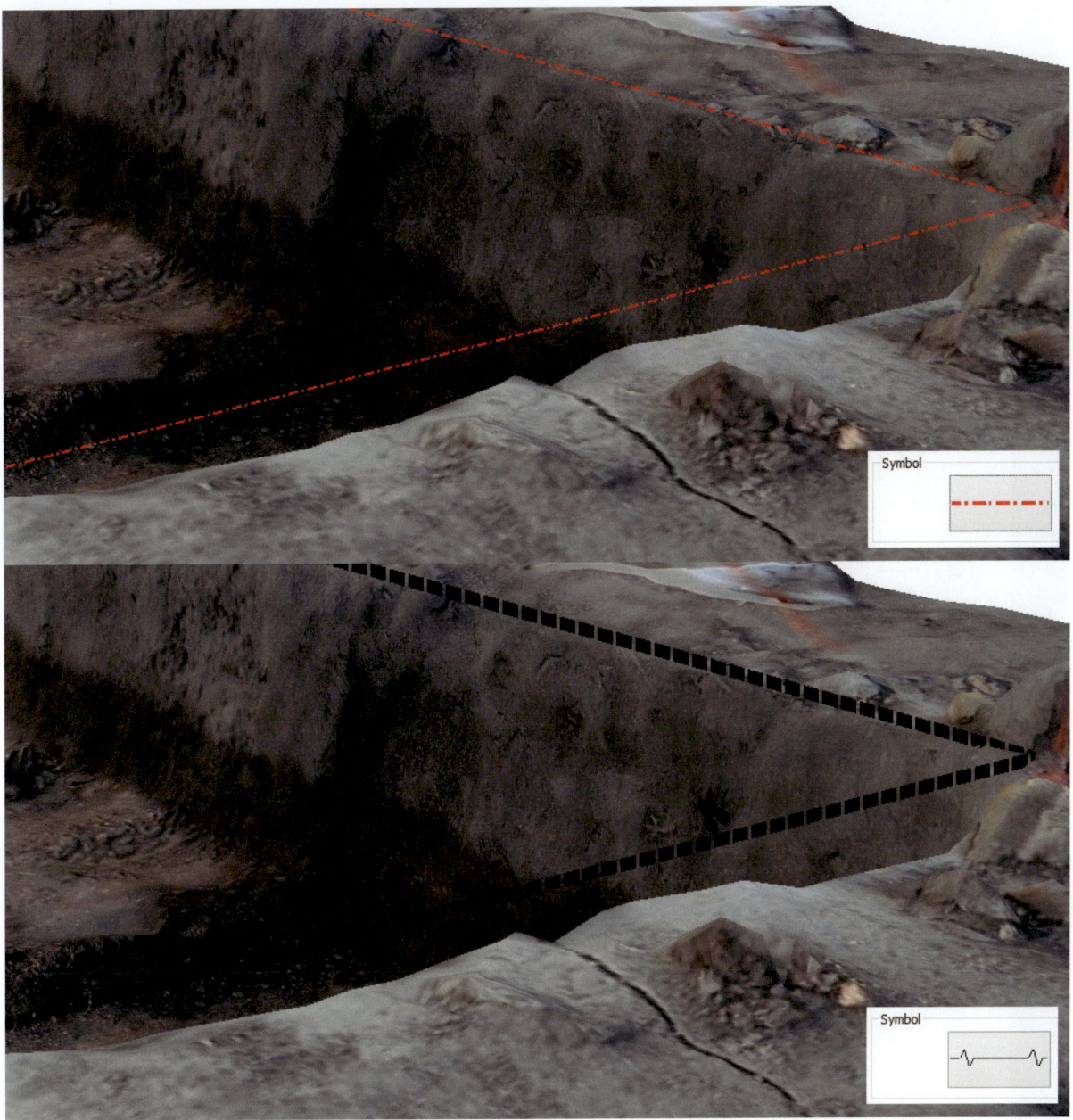

FIGURE 30 – (COMPOSITE SCREEN-CAPTURE OF 3D MODELS) SHOWN HERE IS HOW ARCSCENE PROJECTS LINES. THE TOP IMAGE IS A SIMPLE LINE THAT IS EASILY PROJECTED; BOTTOM IS A COMPLEX LINE WHICH ARCSCENE CANNOT PROJECT. FOR BOTH IMAGES, THE CORRESPONDING LINE SYMBOLOGY IS DENOTED IN THE BOTTOM RIGHT CORNER OF THE RELATED IMAGE (IMAGE BY J.J.L. KIMBALL 2014; 3D MODELS BY J.J.L. KIMBALL).

in mind, one can achieve a great amount with only the most basic types of lines. Thus, in response to this matter, I have translated only the simplest of lines over to ESRI's ArcScene for use in 3D drawing (FIGURE 31). These lines represent important archaeological knowledge that must be presented as part of any graphical representation package. Ideally, we should be able to translate the entire palette of line types from the single context method into a 3D GIS platform like ArcScene. Until that happens, however, the basic line types, used in unison with attribute tables and unique perspectives, will have to suffice.

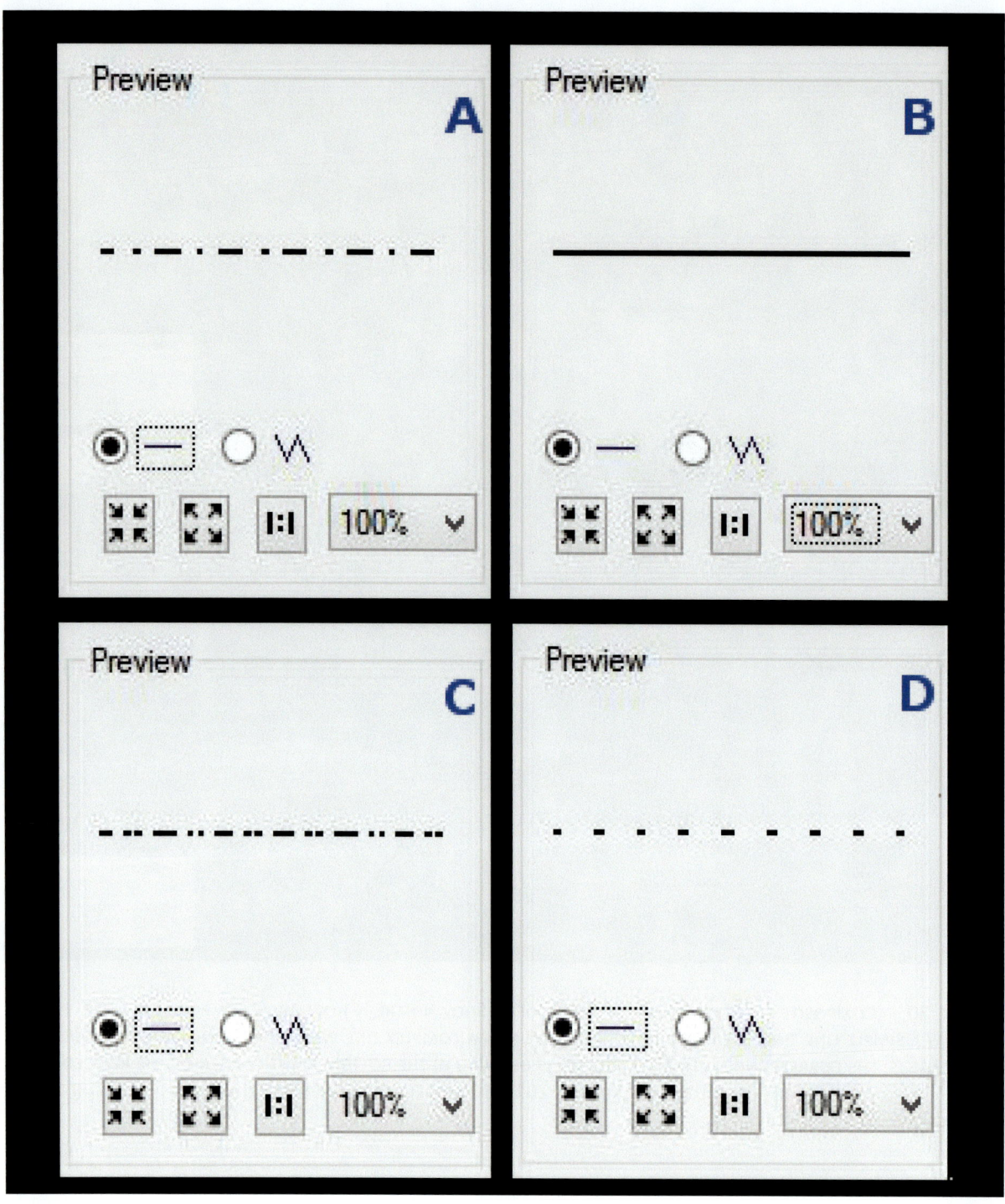

FIGURE 31 – A PROPOSED STANDARD SYMBOLOGY FOR 3D DRAWING: (A) LIMIT OF EXCAVATION; (B) EXTENT OF CONTEXT; (C) EDGE OF CONTEXT TRUNCATED BY LATTER INTRUSION; AND (D) EXTENT UNCERTAIN. (IMAGE BY J.J.L. KIMBALL 2014).

6.2 – Cautions and Limitations

As grand and visually impressive as 3D models are and impressive their applications may be, it must be stressed that, as documentative and interpretative tools, *they are only as effective as those other tools that are used in concert alongside them*. This statement has been a central theme throughout this work and it is an important caution to bear in mind specifically towards 3D digital technologies and even more generally in regards to any form of technology. Archaeology is as much an art as it is a science—both of which are invested in developing as clear, concise, and informative a picture as possible—and archaeologists accomplish this by using a variety of tools to gather a number of perspectives that together help to enrich our understanding of the past. In this sense, archaeology may be considered more akin to a craft skill (Edgeworth 2006: 77). This concept can be illustrated with the experiences garnered throughout the writing process of this work.

At the beginning, before I had access to the formal archaeological site report or the excavation GIS,[5] I was restricted to the photographs and the 3D models derived through MSR from those photographs. When I started to experiment with my drawing techniques in ArcGIS, I quickly realised that I could identify archaeological contexts and features—but had absolutely no idea, at least beyond speculation based on experience, what they may be and how they could have been related. Furthermore, I had no way of knowing whether there were any 'invisible' contexts—those that are not so apparent with the eye, but are very much so 'felt' with the trowel (since 3D models are *visual* representations, drawing a context where the quality of the soil was 'felt' to be dramatically different than the surrounding soil is impossible without documentation or personally experiencing the excavation).

Fortunately, I was granted access to all the information I needed, however, this experience has influenced me to share this caution about 3D—or for that matter, any other—documentative technology. Such technologies, however powerful they may be, are only useful when operated in concert with other documentation formats. 3D models and the ability to draw in 3D upon those models represents only one means to study the archaeological excavation—it enriches other perspectives, but it is also itself enriched by those other perspectives. Another point to stress is one discussed in the subsection immediately above: these techniques are also constricted by the knowledge of the user. Therefore, such documentation methodologies must absolutely be applied whenever possible by those who are actually in the field performing the excavations. The archaeologist who digs a specific trench has an intimate knowledge that is accessible only by her/him. While a GIS technician can undoubtedly make such 3D drawings and connect them into the database, the archaeologist that possess that intimate knowledge might be able to do so with more precision and/or description exactly because of that knowledge and first-hand experience.

There may also be some concern regarding the nature behind the act of drawing in 3D over top of 3D models—that this process is itself purely interpretative rather than observational. The issue therefore is that, as an interpretative medium, 3D drawing cannot be a form of objective documentation. There is of course a level of truth to the above apprehension. What must be kept in mind, however, is that archaeologists are constantly and actively interpreting things that diverge from a perceived norm. This exemplifies exactly what Hodder has argued: that the act of excavation is itself the act of interpretation (1999: 83). Each excavation is unique (e.g. the archaeology itself is different, what resources are available, the level of urgency to excavate, the skill of the excavators, and so on). Archaeologists therefore must pose appropriate questions and goals for each excavation and determine what methodologies will produce

---

[5] I would like to stress that I intend absolutely no disrespect to the excavation leaders, my supervisor, or anyone else with access to the archaeological documentation from Uppåkra. These individuals were accommodating and extremely generous in providing me access to any and all of the materials I required or, at the very least, guided me to an individual who had access. My intentions with this paragraph have been to demonstrate a potential, but very serious, limitation to the technologies I have used and techniques I have developed for this work.

the best results. This is reflected in documentation methodology where archaeologists actively choose—or *interpret*—the moment *when* to engage in record-making and *through what technology* that record is accomplished. This problem resonates with the problem that Hodder notes, that archaeologists too readily refuse to acknowledge that the practice of archaeology—including the act of documentation—is theoretical and therefore, through design and perspective, it is also *interpretative* (Hodder 1999: 81-82).

The above paragraph highlights an important discussion in archaeology today where archaeological data is coming under scrutiny to determine whether it is objective or constructive. Unfortunately, this is an issue that far surpasses what the scope this work is capable of achieving. However, it is important to take a stance on the matter. Perhaps it is most useful to seek a solution by understanding the definition of a document, which is defined by the *Oxford Dictionary of English* as "a piece of written, printed, or electronic matter that *provides information or evidence or that serves as an official record*" [emphasis mine] (Stevenson 2010). Archaeologists, over the course of the excavation, are constantly producing such documentation that can be argued as being more or less affected by interpretation. Photo-realistic 3D models are a 'real' representation of the archaeology uncovered while a 3D drawing is more of a representation of what the archaeologist has deemed as important. While there may be a clear distinction between the two formats here, what is most important to recognise is that both formats are capturing, containing, and displaying data that has been deemed as important. It is therefore arguable that 3D drawings can and should be considered as a valid form of documentation that can enrich the understanding of an archaeological site during and after the excavation process.

Moving on, there is a particularly rather inconvenient limitation of using ESRI's ArcGIS for this methodology that became apparent during the experiment—there is no easy way to view the 3D archaeological drawings in 3D outside of ArcGIS. It is possible to export specific perspectives in popular 2D file formats (such as PDF, JPG, and TIFF), but the only way to export the 3D drawings as 3D representations is through a vector format type file ending with 'WRL' (or the updated version VRML, both referring to Virtual Reality Modelling Language). This is problematic for two reasons: first is that specialist software is needed to visualise this file format and even when specialist software is downloaded, the visualisation of the data through the WRL file is difficult to 'explore' on-screen; and second is that as a vector file format, WRL does not allow for the visualisation of the raster components of the 3D model. Thus, WRL is an inefficient file format for the exportation of these 3D models and their associated data. Whether this issue is being addressed by ESRI is unknown to the author, as is whether other GISs with 3D visualisation capabilities are able to perform the exportation of 3D documents. Considering that the PDF file format has the capability to visualise 3D data, it is my hope that ESRI will in the future include an export option to do so. In the meantime, future endeavours to uncover a manner of visualising these data are an absolute requirement for the dissemination value of this methodology. Until then, the only feasible manner of disseminating this information is through ArcGIS itself which carries with it obvious negative factors (e.g. especially price of the software itself and the weight (in GB or gigabytes) of the 3D document).

An even more frustrating issue with ESRI's ArcScene was the difficulties that were experienced by the operator when attempting to draw upon a vertically oriented surface. As noted in *Section 5.6* of this work, at best there was some discrepancy with how shapefile nodes were placed upon a vertical surface. At worst, however, was concerning how polygons were projected where a single polygon (intended to be one polygon) was broken apart into sometimes incoherent structures barely reminiscent of the pattern of nodes laid down (FIGURE 32; cf. also FIGURE 18, FIGURE 19, and FIGURE 20 above). It is suspected that these problems rest within the software itself and that in the future they will be addressed by ESRI. Regardless, at the time of writing this work, it is an important limitation that must be acknowledged particularly in that it limits how much an archaeologist can do with this technique for now. Once this issue has been dealt with, the value of this technique, or others like, it will undoubtedly result in more of an impact within archaeology.

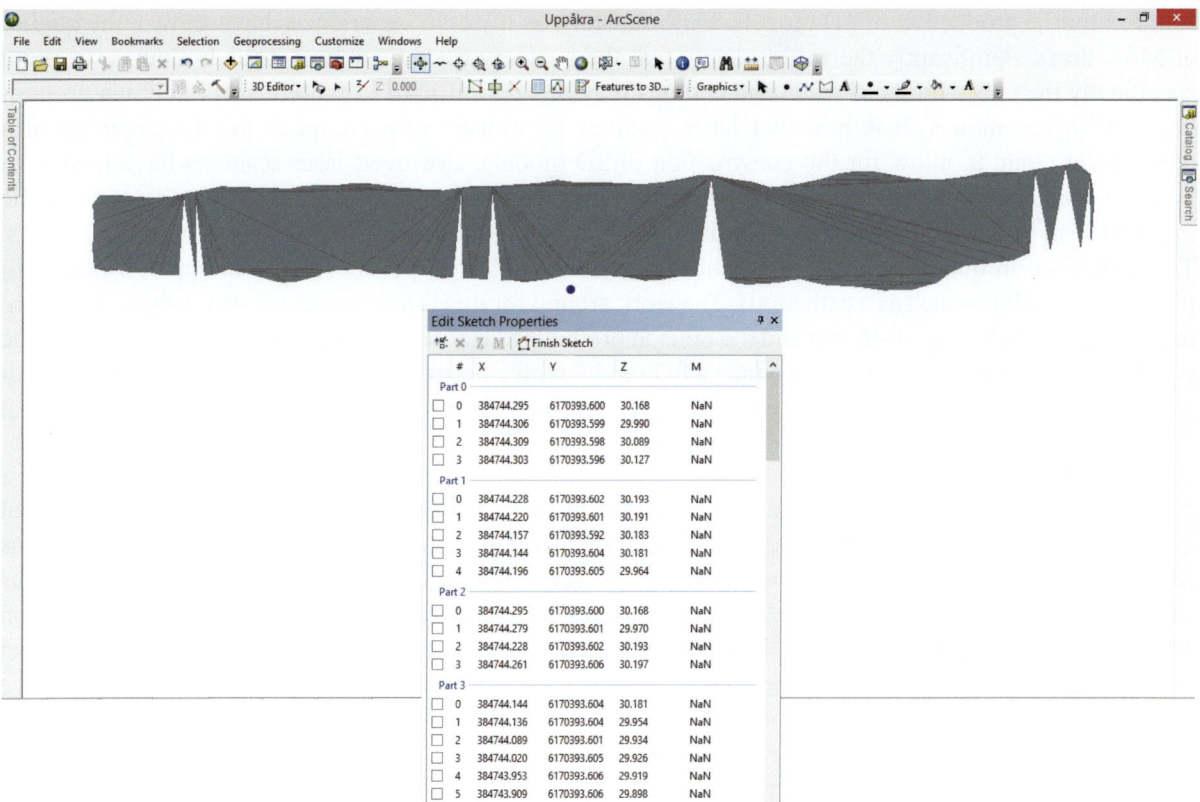

FIGURE 32 – (SCREEN-CAPTURE OF 3D DRAWING) DESPITE PLACING THE NODES IN A LOGICAL SEQUENCE, THE RESULTING POLYGON IS NOT CORRECTLY PROJECTED. INSTEAD OF A SINGLE POLYGON, ARCSCENE BREAKS IT INTO NINE DIFFERENT PIECES OR 'PARTS'—EACH WITH ITS OWN SPECIFIC SET OF NODES. (IMAGE BY J.J.L. KIMBALL 2014; 3D MODEL/3D DRAWING BY J.J.L. KIMBALL 2014).

Another problem with ESRI's ArcScene that is worth mentioning is that there is no way to add legends, grids, or scale bars. Considering that archaeological imagery is often accompanied by a combination of these three items, this may be a particularly significant drawback. Speculation suggests that the reason the legend, grid, and scale bar items have been omitted from ArcScene relates to the fact that, like the 2D lines spoken about before, these items do not easily translate from 2D items into 3D items. After all, ArcScene is itself a 3D visualisation platform so it is questionable how useful static 2D objects, such as these, would be as one shifted their perspective about the scene in complex manners. There is little doubt that the exclusion of these three important items can be detrimental to the value of these models and drawings—especially when it is necessary to present them upon a 2D medium (e.g. paper). While there are work-around techniques for these (e.g. using the measuring tool in ArcScene in lieu of the scale bar, constructing a grid with polylines, or creating a legend for the symbols in an image editing software), it would be useful perhaps that in the future ESRI developed some way of dealing with these issues. Perhaps a 2D overlay option to display the legend so that no matter how one moves the camera in the scene, the legend stays statically projected. As for the scale bar, perhaps ESRI can develop a 3D scale bar that can be placed and oriented in the scene (in the same manner that a range pole is used in archaeological photography). Unfortunately, until a solution allowing for these items to be projected within ArcScene is found, archaeologists will either have to make do without or construct their own solutions.

It is my sincerest wish that the methodology developed for this work is considered by many of the archaeological sub-disciplines. However, I must strongly advise that for some archaeological applications (in particular for example, buildings archaeology or landscape archaeology), MSR might not be a feasible solution for the production of 3D models. Unfortunately, as my own experiences have shown, the quality of MSR drops significantly the further away that the subject of acquisition is. Thus buildings, or more specifically the upper limits of walls and ceilings may be very difficult to capture accurately via ground-based MSR techniques. It is best that laser scanners be utilised to accomplish the development of a dense point cloud to allow for the construction of 3D models. However, laser scanners have their own inherent problems. Most problematic is that, while laser scanners do have a digital camera to assist in the production of photo-realistic textures for the model, these digital cameras pale in comparison to DSLRs. The difference in quality is most pronounced when the subject is poorly lit (for example, a poorly-lit interior of a building such as a cathedral). The work around for this is to conduct two campaigns in unison: one aiming at producing MSR data and the other at producing laser scanner data. One can then combine the two typologies of data in order to produce a 3D model with extremely high-quality geometry and photo-realistic textures. These 3D models can then be input into GIS and used to perform 3D archaeological drawings in the manner suggested by this work.

I would now like to bring to the reader's attention to two final points for contemplation. First is that archaeologists must strive to remember that these 3D technologies produce very persuasive representations of the world around us. A famous quote, coined by Alfred Korzybski and analysed by Gregory Bateson, is of particular relevance: *the map is not the territory mapped, and the name is not the thing named* (Bateson 1979: 30). Consequentially, this can be further expanded to state that the photograph is not the subject photographed and the *3D model is not the thing modelled*. It is therefore a serious oversight to believe that these ways of representing our perceived world are anything more than representations. After all, it is us ourselves whom must decide or *interpret* what is worthwhile to capture as well as when, why, and how we that subject should be captured. In short, the resulting representations must therefore be treated accordingly. Second is that the institutions of higher learning that are responsible for educating the next generation of archaeologists must be active in teaching students not just how to use these technologies, but also the foundations upon which they are built. In this manner, it is possible today to ensure a higher quality of archaeological documentation in the future.

If anything is to be taken away from these cautions and limitations it is that: 1) 3D digital documentation technologies cannot be used as the sole documentary method—they must be used in unison with other formats to ensure that a rich, detailed, and (most importantly) archaeologically-relevant dataset can be achieved from the excavation; and 2) whenever possible, the act of drawing upon the 3D models, must be undertaken by the archaeologist that was involved with the process of excavation—as only they, through their direct and developed interpretations, can ensure that the most accurate interpretation of the archaeology presented through those drawings. If these two considerations are met, then it is possible to ensure that these techniques and technologies are utilised in the most appropriate manner for archaeological investigation.

6.3 – Concerns Regarding the Photographic Process

Before the close of this work it is important to discuss some concerns regarding the current photographic process within archaeological practice—specifically for application within the MSR technique. In response to the digitisation of camera technologies, archaeologists should consider re-evaluating the process and guidelines for archaeological photography. While discussing the entire matter is well beyond the scope of this work, an attempt has been made to briefly address the photographic process as it is conducted in the MSR technique. Other researchers have already discussed the need for careful photography when utilising MSR and MSR-like approaches for the creation of 3D models. While I respect much of what has been emphasised by these researchers, I want to suggest some amendments to the current photographic method as I believe there is room for improvement. It has been rightly cautioned that the quality of model output from the MSR technique is dependent upon the quality of data input: in other words, impressive visual

3D representations require high-quality, high-resolution, and very sharp (in-focus) photographs. Chapman (2009: 54) points out that GIS databases are only as good as the data input—the same holds true for 3D digital models produced through MSR. The following paragraphs will address some of the issues that must be considered regarding the photographic process in archaeology.

Prior to any photographs being captured of the site, archaeologists must first pay close attention to the preparation of both the site itself and the archaeological surfaces within. By design, photographs record all visible entities that are in their field of view—this often leads to clutter and a weakening of the message that the photographer is trying to convey through her/his photograph. It is for this very reason that professional photographers commonly state that *photography is the art of exclusion*—or in other words, the photograph should focus on and contain only the intended subject of capture. This very endeavour is critical for archaeological photography too, in that care must be taken to remove items that are non-essential to the photographic record of the site (e.g. buckets, shovels, trowels, measuring sticks, kneepads, etc.) (Fisher 2009: 13). However, in respect to photography aimed at the development of 3D models, it is just as important to (temporarily) remove other items such as strings that delineate boundaries, small finds markers that protrude from the surface being photographed, and even prominent trench markers such as range poles. All of these items lead towards cluttering the resulting digital model and can even negatively impact the end product (FIGURE 33 and FIGURE 34), and therefore it is important to remove them whenever possible. Another task that must be accomplished is that the archaeological surfaces must be properly prepared for documentation. This involves trowelling away a very thin layer off the surface. Such a procedure can be termed a 'photo-clean' of the surface and while there are variations in method depending on the material encountered, all methods are aimed at clearing away anything that obstructs (e.g.

FIGURE 33 – (PHOTOGRAPH) BUCKETS, STRINGS, FINDS MARKERS, RANGE POLES—ALL OF THESE MUST BE CLEARED FROM THE SITE TO ENSURE AS CLEAN A MODEL AS POSSIBLE. (PHOTOGRAPH © J.J.L. KIMBALL 2013).

FIGURE 34 – (SCREEN-CAPTURE OF A 3D MODEL) THE CONSEQUENCE OF NOT PREPARING THE SITE BY REMOVAL OF ITEMS NON-ESSENTIAL FOR THE PHOTOGRAPHIC PROCESS. VISIBLE ARE MULTIPLE PROJECTIONS OF ONE STRING, A NEON STRIP OF TAPE, AND A HINT OF RED IN THE CORNER OF THE TRENCH FROM A RANGE POLE. (IMAGE BY J.J.L. KIMBALL 2014; 3D MODEL BY J.J.L. KIMBALL 2014).

loose spoil, boot prints, etc.) the underlying archaeology (FIGURE 35). A proper cleaning of the surface also has the effect of 'freshening' the site, making some context extents appear crisper and producing a more vivid distinction between colours (Barker 1993: 108-109; Fisher 2009: 13; Roskams 2001: 126-128). It is crucial that the site be properly prepared for documentation in these manners. Not only does it contribute to the production of very crisp archaeological photographs, but these photographs in turn will result in excellent geometries and textures for 3D models. While these two benefits should be persuasive enough, it is also pertinent to mention that models with crisp textures facilitates the process of developing 3D archaeological drawings—the more clearly the archaeologist can see the features, the more accurate and efficient she/he will be at producing the drawing.

Another consideration towards site photography is concerning photographic platforms. Any photographer will teach that the most sure-fire way to ensure the capture of sharp images is by stabilising the camera on a sturdy base, such as a tripod. The methodology suggested by many of the research papers, however, omit any mention of a stabilisation platform for the camera—instead opting for the archaeologist to hand-hold the camera and move around the subject. Understandably, in some circumstances, this may be the only option; especially when the lack of time is a particular factor of concern. Yet there are two advantages provided by the use of a tripod. First is that, as a stabilisation

DISCUSSION

FIGURE 35 – (SCREEN-CAPTURE OF A 3D MODEL) THE BLUE CIRCLE HIGHLIGHTS A PARTIAL BOOT PRINT THAT IS FOREVER IMMORTALISED IN THIS 3D DIGITAL MODEL. (IMAGE BY J.J.L. KIMBALL 2014; 3D MODEL BY N. DELL'UNTO).

tool, the tripod allows the photographer to utilise slower shutter speeds and narrower apertures. Such settings therefore enable the capture of very crisp photographs where the plane of focus is deeper and, therefore, less apparent. In contrast, a wide-open aperture lets more light into the camera sensor, thereby allowing for faster shutter speeds (and possibly justifying the methodology to handhold the camera). There is a downside in that wide-open apertures result in photographs with shallow depths of field. What this means is that the plane of focus becomes apparent much more quickly so that objects in the fore- and backgrounds appear out of focus nearer to the plane of focus. This may compound the model construction process, especially in items that are captured in close proximity to the camera, by requiring more photos to be captured with a greater percentage of overlap.

Second is that the tripod itself slows down the photographer—the act of moving the tripod about forces the photographer to experience the scene—to think about the subject—and thus plan the best course of action for photographically acquiring it. Handholding the camera might be quicker, but there is a sense of hurriedness when wielding the camera in this manner. This in turn may result in even the most experienced photographer getting jittery and moving ever so slightly during the capture of photos. Such movement can prove later on to be disastrous for the development of the 3D model, particularly if the opportunity for acquisition has passed. Frustratingly, our modern technological culture has taught us to expect immediate results, and photography is certainly a clear example of this. Photographs in the days of film were carefully planned out and executed, for there were only so many photos one could take before running the risk of expending all the frames in a film cartridge. Today, digital memory cards can hold thousands of photographs, and thus a single photograph does not carry the same amount of necessitated intent and planning as before. If the archaeologist is not careful, there is a very real risk of becoming disconnected from the subject being captured, potentially resulting in carelessness and even confusion towards what was captured and why. A tripod therefore may help, even within the modern state of instant photography, to help bring thoughtfulness and intent back into excavation photography.

Apart from using a tripod there must also be an awareness towards how the digital camera works. Too frequently do we depend solely on our technology working and producing what we expect it to. As stated above, we must understand how we can achieve the results we want—we must pay homage to the traditional technologies and the methods used to achieve the desired results. One of the fundamental tenets of the MSR technique is that, like the aim of drawing features or photographing them, it represents our interpretation that the captured state of the site is actually worth documenting. In other words, we chose to document the archaeology at this particular moment because of something perceived as being archaeologically-relevant. Thereby it is best to capture the site *as we actively see it*, meaning we must capture it in the photographic conditions that are present at that very moment (e.g. lightning, moisture level of the soil, etc.). It is advocated by others that the photographs must not be edited as doing so may misrepresent how the site was actually seen. Yet, there is an issue with this logic. Experience with photographic image formats suggests that, if these files were to be utilised in the time frame of the excavation, compressed image formats, such as JPG, will have likely been utilised over non-compressed, unadulterated RAW forms. The issue with the JPG format is that many cameras, including DSLRs, are programmed to edit the JPGs image when they are captured. In this manner, the camera—not the photographer—is altering certain photographic properties, such as the values of contrast and colour saturation. Photography, no matter the goal, is a type of archaeological documentation and it must therefore be conducted in such a manner by a trained individual. Allowing the camera to oversaturate and/or increase the contrast beyond what was actually seen only does a disservice to the documentation process. Archaeologists must return to the care that was exercised when photography was limited by film. It is now too easy and common practice to assume the camera will do all of the work.

The best method is therefore for the photographer to edit her/his own photographs. Since JPG both edits and compresses the image, a different format must be utilised: RAW. The RAW format functions closest to how film operated in that it is the most unaltered version of the photograph. Like film, the RAW photograph must be developed by a software like Photoshop or GIMP. Unlike permitting the camera itself to determine the edits made, the archaeologist using software like Photoshop has complete control over the editing process and can ensure that only the closest approximation in colour saturation and contrast is applied to the photograph. By utilising a software like Adobe Photoshop Lightroom these edits are easy to achieve and, as is the nature of MSR photography, groups of photographs needing the same modifications can be done all at once, with the result of expediting the process dramatically. All of these software allow for the RAW files to be exported *controllably* into a more storage-friendly format such as JPG. One final comment should be made regarding the RAW and JPG formats: in some circumstances, especially in the methodologies above that advocate for the application of MSR techniques within the timeframe of the excavation, processing the RAW files might not be feasible. Again, a solution is, however, that many DSLR cameras allow for the simultaneous capture of RAW and JPG formats at the same time. While this does take up more memory card space, it does offer the opportunity for the archaeologist to develop a 3D model for immediate application when needed with the ability of developing something closer to reality later (e.g. for publication or for museum display).

7 – Conclusion

This work has set out to explore the implications that new technologies, such as 3D digital models created through the MSR technique, might have for field archaeology. Technology is under constant innovation; old technologies are upgraded into more-advanced and powerful versions, whereas on occasion an entirely unique, unexpected technology is dreamt-up and introduced. Furthermore, an ever-increasing reality needs to acknowledge that these technologies are omnipresent in almost every aspect of our lives. The appropriate response is to avoid remaining ignorant to technology and its applications. Yet, we must also exercise caution and avoid simply accepting technology for the sake of it. Instead, it is becoming necessary to move beyond simply embracing technology and towards developing intelligent, useful, and impacting applications that increase and benefit our interaction and experiences within the world around us. It is with this insight in mind that this work has focused upon a recent methodology concerning the creation of a 3D/4D GIS via MSR techniques. While on its own the use of this methodology affirms that 3D models are capable of disseminating important archaeological information, a need was identified to further explore ways in which to make these models even more relevant to archaeological needs—especially within the timeframe of the actual process of excavation. The goal of this work was to specifically answer the question: in what manners can 3D models be used in the comprehension, interpretation, and visualisation of those materials deemed to be archaeologically relevant?

What was revealed through the experiment was that the traditional two-dimensional approach to archaeological drawing can be accomplished within a three-dimensional space. The key is to give thoughtful and intentional consideration to the history, method, and purpose behind archaeological drawing. Through such acknowledgement, a direct and purposeful methodology can be developed that affirms the relevance of 3D models and 3D documentation techniques for archaeological research. The combination of seeing a photo-realistic 3D representation and drawing in 3D upon that representation obviates the need for traditional line symbols intended as a translation medium for 3D features into 2D information. Furthermore, the act of creating these drawings inside of a GIS is itself important in that they can be appropriated with database attributes allowing for their inclusion in database queries seeking specific attributes. The act of 3D drawing within a GIS, allows for the traditional forms of archaeological drawing—plan and section—to be visualised together at the same time and in the same space. Furthermore, these drawings can be chronologically layered providing that their source material—the 3D models themselves—are captured and included within the GIS in such a manner. This allows for the 'peeling' of both archaeological layers and drawings to reveal the chronological progression in a new manner. Another finding is that these drawings and their associated models can be converted into a variety of file formats (both 2D and 3D) that allow for the dissemination of information amongst archaeologists and non-archaeologists alike. Finally, all of these techniques and methodologies can be accomplished within the timeframe of an ongoing archaeological field investigation.

While the findings detailed above are certainly impressive, their presence together suggests that 3D digital documentation technologies represent a very fruitful and impacting presence in field archaeology. Thus I have proposed that archaeologists begin to consider techniques involving 3D models, such as 3D archaeological drawing, as the future direction for archaeology. I have suggested in *6.1 - Statement of Perceived Impact* that those typologies of approaches should be a step towards updating the archaeological method of drawing. By this, I do not advocate that 3D drawings should supplant the traditional methodology, but instead that this technique should be acknowledged as the *technological evolution* of the archaeological drawing. By conducting such techniques in a 3D digital medium, we are not only engaging more deeply with the omnipresence of technology—we are documenting directly in the format that we actively experience archaeology as it exists in the real world. To phrase it more simply and eloquently, *we are engaging 3D problems with 3D solutions*. Archaeologists today, as capable of advocating change for present and future archaeological endeavours, must begin to concern themselves with the modernisation of the archaeological discipline. The embracement and continual development of 3D models and their associated techniques is an example of one potential direction that may contain many fruitful prospects for such an undertaking.

Yet there are limitations that must be kept ever-present in the mind. 3D models and 3D drawing cannot be used as the only form of documentation. It is necessary to remember that these documentation formats are part of an interconnected and interdependent web of many documentation types that, as a whole, strengthen each other and create a more vivid picture of the past. As such, it must be ensured that this technology is employed by the most qualified individual—the archaeologist that actually performed the excavation. Only she/he understands and can reiterate the story of how the excavation had progressed. If they are not allowed to document their interpretations of the archaeology through the methodologies defined above, then the documentation itself suffers in quality. Finally, it is important to remember that the 3D models themselves are not the subject modelled—in other words, models are not 'truths'. 3D models are extremely powerful and they are powerful to the point that they are persuasive and enchanting. It must always be remembered that they are interpretations and must be relegated within the role of helping to understand archaeological knowledge as opposed to dictating it.

When utilised properly, however, 3D replicas of the site offer a plethora of uses. While I have striven to produce as full and thoughtful of a methodology as possible, there will always be room for improvement. Future research can definitely be aimed towards refining the technique above or discovering alternate methods altogether. Another direction of interest would be to explore further other applications that 3D models may have for archaeological research. It is, after all, worthwhile to define what 3D models are and are not capable of. Only through such scrutiny can their true value be realised and their proper place defined within archaeological research.

What is important to take away from this work is that the technologies and methodologies as described above are all capable of impacting archaeological research *within the timeframe of the process of excavation* in profound manners. Archaeologists do a disservice to the discipline by clinging stubbornly to technologies of the past. Yet the same can be stated for those archaeologists who embrace modern technology for the sake of embracing it. Instead, what archaeologists must strive for is a way to acknowledge the history of archaeological practice as a means to justify and cement the adoption of new technology. As a result, we can then move towards upgrading or modernising the traditional technologies and methodologies of the excavation process. Through such actions, we ensure that the act of archaeological investigation is maintained and kept efficient, but it also enables us to upgrade the archaeological toolkit with more sophisticated tools that not only allow for us to develop a larger and more clear picture of the past but, more importantly, permit us to arrive at new and exciting questions that ensure the continuation and future evolution of archaeological endeavours.

8 – Acknowledgments

I would like to take a brief moment to extend my appreciation towards my supervisor, Nicolo Dell'Unto, for the support, guidance, and patience throughout the past two years, and for granting me access to the models and data he collected himself from the Uppåkra excavations. To Jan Apel, thank you first and foremost for allowing me use to the excavation's drawings and records, but also for the feedback and suggested future considerations regarding this work. To Carolina Larsson and Stefan Lindgren, I would like to express my thanks for your support in all technological matters—your assistance throughout the year with various quirks and problems relating to 3D models has been extremely helpful. Thank you also to Birgitta Piltz Williams for taking the time to accommodate both my photo and geospatial acquisition campaigns during a very busy dig season in 2013.

To all of the professors and instructors whom I have had the opportunity of learning from over these past two years, you have my sincerest gratitude—there is no doubt in my mind that my colleagues and I have benefitted immensely from your willingness to share with us your collective knowledge and experiences.

Last but certainly not least, to all my fellow colleagues, friends, mentors, and family members: you are most definitely not forgotten nor unappreciated. On the contrary, the largest and most resounding thanks must go to you, for if not for your collective support, patience, advice, wisdom, and laughter, this work would not have been possible.

—— *Tack så mycket, kiitos paljon, thank you!* ——

9 – References

9.1 – Literary Sources

Apel, J. and Piltz Williams, B. 2014. *Uppåkra 2013*. Institutionen för Arkeologi och Antikens Historia, Sweden.

Backhouse, P. 2006. Drowning in data? Digital data in a British contracting unit. In T. L. Evans and P. Daly (eds.) *Digital Archaeology: bridging method and theory*: 43-49. Routledge, United Kingdom.

Balzani, M., Santopuoli, N., Grieco, A., and Zaltron, N. 2004. Laser Scanner 3D Survey in Archaeological Field: the Forum of Pompeii. *International Conference on Remote Sensing Archaeology*: 169-175.

Barker, P. 1993. *Techniques of Archaeological Excavation*. Routledge, United Kingdom.

Callieri, M., Dell'Unto, N., Dellepiane, M., Scopigno, R., Soderberg, B., and Larsson, L. 2011. Documentation and Interpretation of an Archaeological Excavation: an experience with Dense Stereo Reconstruction tools. *The 12th International Symposium on Virtual Reality, Archaeology and Cultural Heritage VAST*.

Campana, S. 2014. 3D Recording and Modelling in Archaeology and Cultural Heritage: Theory and best practices. In F. Remondino and S. Campana (eds.) *3D Recording and Modelling in Archaeology and Cultural Heritage: Theory and best practices*: 7-12. BAR International Series 2598.

Cianciarulo, D. and Guerra, F. 2007. Digital Recording in Archaeological Excavation Using Tablet PC. *XXI International CIPA Symposium, 01-06 October, Athens, Greece*.

Conolly, J. and Lake, M. 2006. *Geographical Information Systems in Archaeology*. Cambridge University Press, United Kingdom.

Cummer, W. W. 1974. Photogrammetry at Ayia Irini on Keos. *Journal of Field Archaeology*, 1 (3/4): 385-387.

De Reu, J., De Smedt, P., Herremans, D., Van Meirvenne, M., Laloo, P., and De Clercq, W. 2014. On introducing an image-based 3D reconstruction method in archaeological excavation practice. *Journal of Archaeological Science*, 41: 251-262.

Dellepiane, M., Dell'Unto, N., Callieri, M., Lindgren, S., and Scopigno, R. 2013. Archeological excavation monitoring using dense stereo matching techniques. *Journal of Cultural Heritage*, 14 (3): 201-210.

Dell'Unto, N. 2014. The Use of 3D Models for Intra-Site Investigation in Archaeology. In F. Remondino and S. Campana (eds.) *3D Recording and Modelling in Archaeology and Cultural Heritage: Theory and best practices*: 151-158. BAR International Series 2598.

Doneus, M. and Neubauer, W. 2005. 3D Laser Scanners on Archaeological Excavations. *CIPA 2005 XX International Symposium*.

Drewitt, P. L. 2011. *Field Archaeology: An Introduction*. 2nd Edition. Routledge, United Kingdom.

Ducke, B., Score, D., and Reeves, J. 2011. Multiview 3D reconstruction of the archaeological site at Weymouth from image series. *Computers & Graphics*, 35: 375-382.

Edgeworth, M. 2006. *Acts of Discovery: An Ethnography of Archaeological Practice*. Doctoral Thesis. University of Durham, United Kindom.

Eisenbeiss, H. 2009. A Model Helicopter Over Pinchango Alto - Comparison of Terrestrial Laser Scanning and Aerial Photogrammetry. In M. Reindel and G. A. Wagner (eds.) *New Technologies for Archaeology: Multidisciplinary Investigations in Palpa and Nasca, Peru*. Springer, United Kingdom.

Fisher, L. J. 2009. Photography for Archaeologists Part I : Site specific record. *BAJR Practical Guide Series, Guide 25*. British Archaeological Jobs and Resources, United Kingdom.

Fitzjohn, M. 2011. Viewing places: GIS applications for examining the perception of space in the mountains of Sicily. *World Archaeology*, 39 (1): 36-50.

Forte, M. 2014. Virtual Reality, Cyberarchaeology, Teleimmersive Archaeology. In F. Remondino and S. Campana (eds.) *3D Recording and Modelling in Archaeology and Cultural Heritage: Theory and best practices*: 115-129. BAR International Series 2598.

Forte, M., Dell'Unto, N., Issavia, J., Onsureza, L., and Lercaria, N. 2012. 3D Archaeology at Çatalhöyük. *International Journal of Heritage in the Digital Era*, 1 (3): 351-378.

Fussell, A. 1982. Terrestrial photogrammetry in archaeology. *World Archaeology*, 14 (2): 157-172.

Fux, P., Sauerbier, M., Kersten, T., Linstaedt, M., and Eisenbeiss, H. 2009. Perspectives and Constrasts: Documentation and Interpretation of the Petroglyphs of Chichictara, Using Terrestrial Laser Scanning and Image-Based 3D Modeling. In M. Reindel and G. A. Wagner (eds.) *New Technologies for Archaeology: Multidisciplinary Investigations in Palpa and Nasca, Peru*: 359-377. Springer, United Kingdom.

Guidi, G. 2014. Terrestrial Optical Active Sensors—Theory and Applications. In F. Remondino and S. Campana (eds.) *3D Recording and Modelling in Archaeology and Cultural Heritage: Theory and best practices*: 39-62. BAR International Series 2598.

Harris, E. C. 1997. *Principles of archaeological stratigraphy*. 2nd Edition. Academic Press, United Kingdom.

Hermon, S. and Nikodem, J. 2008. 3D Modelling as a Scientific Research Tool in Archaeology. In A. Posluschny, K. Lambers, and I. Herzog (eds.) *Layers of Perception. Proceedings of the 35th International Conference on Computer Applications and Quantitative Methods in Archaeology (CAA), Berlin, Germany, April 2-6 2007 (Kolloquien zur Vor- und Frühgeschichte, Vol 10)*: 1-6.

Hodder, I. 1999. *The Archaeological Process: An Introduction*. Blackwell, United Kingdom.

Hodder, I. (ed.) 2000. *Towards a reflexive method in archaeology: the example at Çatalhöyük*. McDonald Institute for Archaeological Research, United Kingdom.

Jauregui, L. M. and Jauregui, M. 2000. Terrestrial Photogrammetry Applied to Architectural Restoration and Archaeological Surveys. *International Archives of Photogrammetry and Remote Sensing*, XXXIII (B5): 401-405.

Khorram, S., Nelson, S. A. C., Kock, F. H., van der Wiele, C. F. 2012. *Remote Sensing*. Springer, United Kingdom.

Koutsoudis, A., Vidmar, B., Ioannakis, G., Arnaoutoglou, F., Pavlidis, G., and Chamzas, C. 2014. Multi-image 3D reconstruction data evaluation. *Journal of Cultural Heritage*, 15: 73-79.

Kraus, K. 2007. *Photogrammetry: Geometry from Images and Laser Scans*. I. Harley and S. Kyle (trans.) 2nd Edition. Walter de Gruyter GmbH and Co., Germany.

Lagerqvist, B. and Rosvall, J. 2003. A system approach to the management of photographs and other information sources within the conservation field. *Photogrammetric Record*, 18 (102): 105-130.

Larsson, L. 2007. The Iron Age ritual building at Uppåkra, southern Sweden. *Antiquity*, 81: 11-25.

Madry, S., Cole, M., Gould, S., Resnick, B., Seibel, S., and Wilkerson, M. 2005. In M. W. Mehrer and K. L. Wescott (eds.) *GIS and Archaeological Site Location Modeling*: 292-309 Taylor & Francis, United Kingdom.

Mccoy, M. D., Mills, P. R., Lundblah, S., Rieth, T., Kahn, J. G., and Gard, R. 2011. A cost surface model of volcanic glass quarrying and exchange in Hawai'i. *Journal of Archaeological Science*, 38 (10): 2547-2560.

Museum of London Archaeological Service. 1994. *Archaeological Site Manual*. 3rd Edition. RAS Printers Ltd., United Kingdom.

Muzzupappa, M., Gallo, A., Spadafora, F., Manfredi, F., Bruno, F., and Lamarca, A. 2013. 3D reconstruction of an outdoor archaeological site through a multi-view stereo technique. *Digital Heritage International Congress*, 1: 169-176.

Nordbladh, J. 2012. The Shape of History: To give physical form to archaeological knowledge. In O. W. Jensen (ed.) *Histories of Archaeological Practices: Reflections on Methods, Strategies and Social Organisation in Past Fieldwork*. NRS tryckeri, Sweden.

Nylén, E. 1978. The recording of unexcavated finds: X-ray photography and photogrammetry. *World Archaeology*, 10 (1): 88-93.

Owen, O. and Dalland, M. 1999. *Scar: a Viking boat burial on Sanday, Orkney*. Tuckwell, United Kingdom.

Parcak, S. H. 2009. *Satellite Remote Sensing for Archaeology*. Routledge, United Kingdom.
Remondino, F. 2014. Photogrammetry: Theory. In F. Remondino and S. Campana (eds.) *3D Recording and Modelling in Archaeology and Cultural Heritage: Theory and best practices*: 65-73. BAR International Series 2598.
Roskams, S. 2001. *Excavation*. Cambridge University Press, United Kingdom.
Schowengerdt, R. A. 2007. *Remote Sensing: Models and Methods for Image Processing*. 3rd Edition. Academic Press, United States of America.
Szeliski, R. 2011. *Computer Visions: Algorithms and Applications*. Springer, United Kingdom.
Söderberg, B., and Piltz Williams, B. 2012. *Uppåkra 2011*. Institutionen för Arkeologi och Antikens Historia, Sweden.
Söderberg, B., Piltz Williams, B., and Bolander, A. 2014. *Uppåkra 2012*. Institutionen för Arkeologi och Antikens Historia, Sweden.
Stevenson, A. (ed.) 2010. *Oxford Dictionary of English*. 3rd Edition. Oxford University Press, United Kingdom.
Tolkien, J. R. R. 2008. *The Fellowship of the Ring*. Digital Reset Edition. Harper Collins, United Kingdom
Trinks, I., Larsson, L., Gabler, M., Nau, E., Neubauer, W., Klimcyk, A., Söderberg, B., and Thorén, H. 2013. Large-Scale Archaeological Prospection of the Iron Age Settlement Site Uppåkra - Sweden. In W. Neubauer, I. Trinks, R. B. Salisbury, and C. Einwögerer (eds.) *Proceedings of the 10th International Conference on Archaeological Prospection Vienna, May 29th - June 2nd 2013*: 31-34. Austrian Academy of Sciences Press, Austria.
Veljanovski, T. and Stančič, Z. 2005. Predictive Modeling in Archaeological Location Analysis and Archaeological Resource Management: Principles and Applications. In M. W. Mehrer and K. L. Wescott (eds.) *GIS and Archaeological Site Location Modeling*: 363-379. Taylor & Francis, United Kingdom.
Verhoeven, G. 2011. Software Review: Taking Computer Vision Aloft – Archaeological Three-dimensional Reconstructions from Aerial Photographs with Photoscan. *Archaeological Prospection*. 18: 67-73.
Verhoeven, G., Taelman, D., and Vermeulen, F. 2012. Computer Vision-Based Orthophoto Mapping of Complex Archaeological Sites: The Ancient Quarry of Pitaranha (Portugal-Spain). *Archaeometry*, 54 (6): 1114-1129.
Wescott, K. L. 2005. Introduction. In K. L. Wescott and R. J. Brandon (eds.) *Practical Applications of GIS for Archaeologists: A Predictive Modeling Toolkit*: 1-5. Taylor & Francis e-Library Edition. Taylor & Francis, United Kingdom.
Wescott, K. L. and Brandon, R. J. (eds.) 2005. *Practical Applications of GIS for Archaeologists: A Predictive Modeling Toolkit*. Taylor & Francis e-Library Edition. Taylor & Francis, United Kingdom.
Whitley, T. G. 2005. Predictive Modeling in a Homogeneous Environment: An Example from the Charleston Naval Weapons Station, South Carolina. In M. W. Mehrer and K. L. Wescott (eds.) *GIS and Archaeological Site Location Modeling*: 326-361. Taylor & Francis, United Kingdom.
Wiseman, J. R. and El-Baz, F. 2007. Introduction. In J. R. Wiseman and F. El-Baz (eds.) *Remote Sensing in Archaeology*: 1-8. Springer, United States of America.
Wright, D. J., Goodchild, M. F., and Proctor, J. D. 1997. GIS: Tool or Science? Demystifying the Persistent Ambiguity of GIS as "Tool" versus "Science". *Annals of the Association of American Geographers*, 87 (2): 346-362.
Zubrow, E. B. W. 2006. Digital Archaeology: A historical context. In T. L. Evans and P. Daly (eds.) *Digital Archaeology: bridging method and theory*: 8-26. Routledge, United Kingdom.

9.2 – Online Sources

Adobe Systems Incorporated. 2014. Photoshop Lightroom 5: Features. *Adobe*.
[Online] Available from: http://www.adobe.com/products/photoshop-lightroom/features.html [Accessed: 20 Mar 2014].

Agisoft. 2014. Frequently Asked Questions, Agisoft Photoscan: What is the recommended hardware configuration for Photoscan users?. *Agisoft*.
[Online] Available from: http://www.agisoft.ru/support [Accessed: 20 Mar 2014].

Bateson, G. 1979. *Mind and Nature: A Necessary Unity*. E. P. Dutton: United States of America.
[Online] Available from: http://nas.cml-agc.com/public/documents/bateson/mind%20and%20nature%20-%20a%20necessary%20unity.pdf [Accessed: 30 April 2014].

Bennett, B. 2011. Case Study 2. In D. M. Jones (ed.) *3D Laser Scanning for Heritage: Advice and guidance to users on laser scanning in archaeology and architecture*. 2nd Edition.
[Online] Available from: http://www.english-heritage.org.uk/publications/3d-laser-scanning-heritage2/3D_Laser_Scanning_final_low-res.pdf [Accessed: 5 April 2014].

Canon Incorporated. 2014. Canon EOS E550D Product Specification. *Canon*.
[Online] Available from: http://www.canon.co.uk/For_Home/Product_Finder/Cameras/Digital_SLR/EOS_550D/ [Accessed 24 May 2014].

Clarke, J. 2011. Case Study 5. In D. M. Jones (ed.) *3D Laser Scanning for Heritage: Advice and guidance to users on laser scanning in archaeology and architecture*. 2nd Edition.
[Online] Available from: http://www.english-heritage.org.uk/publications/3d-laser-scanning-heritage2/3D_Laser_Scanning_final_low-res.pdf [Accessed: 5 April 2014].

Darvill, T. 2009. The Concise Oxford Dictionary of Archaeology. 2nd Edition. *Oxford Reference*
[Online] Availble from: http://www.oxfordreference.com.ludwig.lub.lu.se/view/10.1093/acref/9780199534043.001.0001/acref-9780199534043-e-231?rskey=vFyzVG&result=2 [Accessed: 11 April 2014].

Davies, T. 2011. Case Study 14. In D. M. Jones (ed.) *3D Laser Scanning for Heritage: Advice and guidance to users on laser scanning in archaeology and architecture*. 2nd Edition.
[Online] Available from: http://www.english-heritage.org.uk/publications/3d-laser-scanning-heritage2/3D_Laser_Scanning_final_low-res.pdf [Accessed: 5 April 2014].

ESRI. 2014. ArcGIS Features. *ESRI*.
[Online] Available from: http://www.esri.com/software/arcgis/features [Accessed: 20 Mar 2014].

Forte, M. 2012. 3D Archaeology at Çatalhöyük. Archaeology of the Mediterranean World.
[Online] Available from: http://mediterraneanworld.wordpress.com/2013/12/05/3d-archaeology-at-catalhoyuk/ [Accessed: 26 April 2014].

Ludwig Botzman Institute for Archaeological Prospection and Virtual Archaeology. 2014. *Ludwig Botzman Institute for Archaeological Prospection and Virtual Archaeology*.
[Online] Available from: http://archpro.lbg.ac.at/ [Accessed: 9 May 2014].

Nikon Corporation. 2008. Total Station: Measuring Distances, Heights, and Angles to Provide Accurate Position Data. *Nikon*.
[Online] Available from: http://www.nikon.com/about/technology/life/others/surveying/index.htm [Accessed: 22 April 2014].

Nikon Corporation. 2014. Nikon Digital SLR Camera D7000 Specifications. *Nikon*.
[Online] Available from: http://imaging.nikon.com/lineup/dslr/d7000/spec.htm [Accessed: 20 March 2014].

Nikon Corporation. 2014a. AF-S DX NIKKOR 10-24mm f/3.5-4.5G ED. *Nikon*.
[Online] Available from: http://imaging.nikon.com/lineup/lens/zoom/widezoom/af-s_dx_10-24mmf_35-45g_ed/index.htm [Accessed: 20 March 2014].

Opitz, R., Terrenato, N., and Limp, F. 2013. Gabii Goes Digital. *Gabii Goes Digital*.
[Online] Available from: http://gabiiserver.adsroot.itcs.umich.edu/gabiigoesdigital/index.html

[Accessed: 9 May 2014].

Prins, A. and Adams, M. J. 2012. Practical Uses for Photogrammetry on Archaeological Excavations. In *JVRP White Papers in Archaeological Technology*.
[Online] Available from: http://www.jezreelvalleyregionalproject.com/practical-uses-for-photogrammetry-on-archaeological-excavations.html [Accessed: 9 May 2014].

Rick, J. W. 1996. Total Stations in Archaeology. *Society for American Archaeology Bulletin*, 14 (4).
[Online] Available from: http://www.saa.org/Portals/0/SAA/publications/SAAbulletin/14-4/SAA16.html [Accessed: 5 April 2014].

Towrie, S. 2014. The Scar Viking Boat Burial. *Orkneyjar: the heritage of the Orkney Islands*.
[Online] Available from: http://www.orkneyjar.com/history/scarboat/ [Accessed: 29 April 2014].

van Maren, G. 2011. 2D to 3D. *ArcGIS Resources*.
[Online] Available from: http://blogs.esri.com/esri/arcgis/2011/09/29/2d-to-3d/ [Accessed: 8 May 2014].

3D Systems. 2014. 3D Scanners: A guide to 3D scanner technology. *3D Systems: Geomagic*.
[Online] Available from: http://www.rapidform.com/3d-scanners/ [Accessed 26 April 2014].

9.3 – Multimedia Sources

Kimball, J. J. L. 2014. Master's Thesis Data.
[Online] Available from: https://sites.google.com/site/justinjlkimball/masters-data [Accessed 28 May 2014].

Kulturhistorisk Museum, UiO. 2014. CfO0166. *Universitetsmuseenes fotoportal*.
[Online] Available from: http://www.unimus.no/foto/imageviewer.html#/?id=12756821&type=jpeg [Accessed 6 May 2014].

Kulturhistorisk Museum, UiO. 2014. CfO0177. *Universitetsmuseenes fotoportal*.
[Online] Available from: http://www.unimus.no/foto/imageviewer.html#/?id=1779938&type=jpeg [Accessed 6 May 2014].